# IT HAPPENED TO ME

## Extraordinary True Stories

### by Ordinary People

**MARTYN FORD**

IT HAPPENED TO ME

Copyright © Martyn Ford 2010

Summersdale Publishers Ltd
46 West Street
Chichester
West Sussex
PO19 1RP
UK

www.summersdale.com

Printed and bound in Great Britain

ISBN: 978-1-84953-016-3

Substantial discounts on bulk quantities of Summersdale books are available to corporations, professional associations and other organisations. For details contact Summersdale Publishers by telephone: +44 (0) 1243771107, fax: +44 (0) 1243 786300 or email: nicky@summersdale.com.

# DISCLAIMER

The opinions expressed in this book are those of the contributors of the stories and not necessarily of Summersdale Publishers Ltd. Should any of the content cause offence or prove inaccurate, it is entirely unintentional and we shall endeavour to make any corrections in future editions.

# CONTENTS

Introduction..................................................................9

Benedict Allen...
... on facing death alone in the Arctic................................11

Ian Colquhoun...
... on losing his legs in an horrific assault........................24

Kerri-Ann Cartwright...
... on winning £2.5 million on The National Lottery...........33

Dave Heeley...
... on running seven marathons, in seven days, on seven continents, despite being blind...............................................39

Kelly Green...
... on being bitten by a brown recluse spider.......................52

John Rose...
... on serving a sentence in one of the world's most savage prisons..................................................................................57

Beverli Rhodes...
... on her escape from the 7 July London bombings...........63

Sinclair Beecham...
... on his rags-to-riches story of founding Pret A Manger....74

Michelle Bowater...

*... on losing fifteen stone to have a baby against all odds....83*

David Tait...

*... on how the abuse he suffered as a child drove him to the top of Everest three times.........................................96*

Craig Green...

*... on beating his near-fatal addiction to heroin................139*

Ann Down...

*... on almost drowning while white-water rafting..............167*

David Stone...

*... on the blood poisoning that nearly killed him...............171*

Kayt Webster-Brown...

*... on being hit by a car..........................................176*

Martin Jones...

*... on losing his sight and then regaining it twelve years later...........................................................182*

Eric Colon...

*... on surviving a wild dog's vicious attack.......................190*

Siobhan Peal...

*... on becoming a woman after living as a man for more than fifty years..............................................195*

Matthew Wood-Hill...

... on surviving prolonged exposure to carbon monoxide...218

Valerie Austin...

... on the amnesia that transformed her life......................224

Lawrence Ford...

... on his bone-shattering arm wrestle................................234

Paul Taylor...

... on accidentally taking a huge dose of LSD....................238

Mark Call...

... on the avalanche that nearly killed him..........................244

Acknowledgements...................................................................253

# INTRODUCTION

This book is a collection of extraordinary true accounts, told to me by those who have experienced what most never will. I set out to gather a diverse selection of pieces and deliberately avoided the tabloid-style horror stories that are often told. I wanted this to be a personal, contextually solid project; the stories here are told in frank detail and I feel the following reflects my intentions. It is for those reasons I have worked hard to keep the stories in the voice of each contributor.

Working closely with those featured in this book has been a pleasure. Far harder was tracking them all down – that's where I spent hours. Now there is a finished product though, full of such a rich variety of people and accounts, it feels like it has been worthwhile.

Some of the stories I have heard during my research for this book have shocked me to the core, some have made me laugh out loud, but all have entertained and all have given me something.

I now find myself wondering more and more what any person on the street might have to tell; what series of events has lead them to this point in their lives and, perhaps most importantly, what wisdom they can pass on.

I have been impressed by people's spirit and resolve in terrible situations that I hope never to experience and their modesty and grace through highs that I hope one day I might. I am left unsure whether these attributes are in us all and emerge when the extreme takes place, or whether only a few possess the courage to push through.

These people are real and I hope the charm and strength of character of all these individuals is conveyed in the following pages.

Putting this book together has been inspiring. Above all else, these pieces have the power to shift everyday concerns and irrelevant worries into perspective and this, I feel, is by far their strongest attribute.

Martyn Ford

# BENEDICT ALLEN...

## ... ON FACING DEATH ALONE IN THE ARCTIC

*'Now I knew I was alone, and that thought seemed to be worse than the realisation that I was going to die out here. My body, my clothes, my dog team, in fact my entire expedition would disappear forever once the ice had melted. There'd be no funeral; no one would even know what had happened to me.'*

I'd been an adventurer for twenty or so years, risked my life a fair bit, but this expedition would take me through an environment far harsher than any I had ever experienced. And that was the whole point in going: I'd learned from a whole range of different indigenous, so-called tribal people how to cope in all manner of environments, most of which were hot.

What excited me about the Russian Far East, though, was that certain villages out in the unforgiving tundra even today rely on traditional dog teams to survive. In fact, whole communities are entirely dependent on their dogs. As someone whose expeditions are about learning skills from people, I was determined to find out more. It's one thing to live in the

Amazon rainforest or Borneo where there's comparatively abundant food, shelter and medicine, or to exist as a nomad herding goats in the desert, but Chukotka is something else. It's a windswept region in the Russian Far East, it's even more remote than Siberia and is perhaps the most hostile environment that man has ever made home.

This adventure would be a personal challenge. In the jungle you can live for perhaps ten days without knowing anything much about survival – the temperatures are moderate and there's usually lots of water. But in the Arctic the line between life and death is very fine indeed. If you fall through the ice, you're dead from a heart attack in maybe a minute. Yet somehow the local people, the Chukchis, have found a way to get by out there in the frozen wastes, herding reindeer in the tundra and hunting seals on the pack ice. I wanted to see if I, too, could learn enough of their skills in order to travel alone with dogs.

My plan was to ask the Chukchis to lend me a dog team, help me train it and then journey 1,000 km north from the regional capital, Anadyr, to a small settlement near the Bering Strait – the 80 km sea between Russia and Alaska. From there I would be on my own. My objective was to continue with my dogs north into the strait and have a go at crossing the pack ice to Alaska. It would be an ambitious project even at the best of times, but nowadays – perhaps due to global warming – the strait only occasionally freezes over in winter. Instead of a nice solid ice bridge, you can expect a mass of shifting ice blocks and turbulent, freezing water.

I soon found that my two Chukchi guides, Yasha and Tolia, as well as being incredibly welcoming and supportive, were very tough indeed. If the temperature was ever as high as -15°C, which it rarely was in winter, they considered the weather balmy and didn't bother to wear gloves. Their dogs seemed to be even tougher! These animals, known as the Chukotka sledge dogs, from which the Siberian husky breed was developed, allow the Chukchis complete mastery of the tundra; a treeless landscape where it's winter much of the year and can be -50°C even without counting the wind chill effect. Chukotka is notoriously windy.

I found the first few days, when I was trying to get to know my dog team in Anadyr, tortuous and thoroughly demoralising. The ten dogs simply refused to obey me. Yasha and Tolia got the same treatment. The dogs were waiting for their master, a man called Alexei, to come back. Meanwhile, they made things as difficult as possible, running this way and that with me on the sledge desperately shouting at them. It didn't help that trying to control the dog rabble on the first day out I got frostbite on all my fingertips.

Adding to my difficulties, this winter (of 2000/2001) was turning out to be the worst in living memory. There were horrendous blizzards and even lower temperatures, though this ironically also gave the best chance in years of a firm ice-bridge building across the strait. Already it had taken three weeks for the weather to clear enough for me to fly into the region and now I was preparing for what seemed a hopelessly overambitious venture in conditions that were testing even for the locals. There were stories of people losing entire limbs to frostbite and two-storey houses being totally buried by the snow.

Eventually, after a few weeks, Yasha and Tolia – characters who thought nothing of working in temperatures that were -80°C with wind chill – decided we'd better make a start on the journey north. They led me off with their own dog teams through the tundra towards my big solo test, the Bering

Strait. This was not only a gruelling journey but also, for me at least, something of a battle of hearts and minds. The dogs were acutely aware of their survival needs but they knew I wasn't competent out here. I'm sure they could even sense I was suffering more than the locals in the cold, gnawing wind that chilled to the bone. The Arctic has a way of sorting the strong from the weak, and the dogs were certainly watching for signs that I was faltering. They knew their lives would depend on their new master and until I'd gained their trust, particularly the trust of the lead dog, they would continue to make it hard for me. Somehow I had to get these dogs on my side and gradually, as we headed nearer and nearer to the strait, time was running out.

Days passed as we worked through the tundra with me yelling 'takh-te' and 'stee-er' – the commands for 'left' and 'right' – and the dogs studiously ignoring me. Gradually the dogs got to know me and, of course, realised that I was now the person feeding them their precious raw walrus, so we began to form a bond. I started to act more efficiently in this environment and I began to understand my dog team and see the part each dog played. The scary character that I called 'Mad Jack' was something of a psychopath but was utterly unafraid of wolves. My lead dog, who I nicknamed 'Top Dog', was small but had that certain mix of intelligence and bravery that made him a natural leader. The huge creature who ran alongside him in the front row was in effect his bodyguard, though all the dogs were well aware of the importance to their own lives of 'Top Dog'. He was the one who steered them away from polar bears and wolves, and prevented them from falling through thin ice or off a cliff.

I said my goodbyes to Yasha and Tolia – they would wait for news of how I was progressing, if at all, in Lorino, their home community. After a final check of my provisions, I strapped my survival kit around my waist and checked over my map again. It was still a further 100 km to the Bering Strait proper and I was very aware that if I got separated from the dogs – if I fell off the sled for example – I wouldn't be coming back. I'd have no communication with the outside world, no satellite phone and no way of getting help. Although my survival kit did include a small stove, allowing me to melt ice to drink, keeping me alive for a few precious hours, the truth was that if I didn't find the sledge quickly I would die, and the death of the dogs would follow soon after. After all, they were harnessed to a hefty sledge carrying my food and gear and also their rations, a stack of raw walrus. So, from that point on, our lives would be totally interdependent. I paused a second, gathering myself, then I gave the dogs the order to set off.

At last, I was alone. This was a moment to be cherished – a scary time, but there was also the exhilaration of knowing that, whether I now failed or succeeded, it was all down to me. All the props had been taken away.

Soon I was heading deep into oblivion, away from the shore and out onto the ice, the frozen sea surface. All around me was the virgin whiteness of the Bering Strait, above me a huge blue, dry sky. I felt very small; it was just me and the ten dogs out here and we were heading further into nowhere.

Sometimes the surface was smooth and all I could hear were the runners of the sledge as we made steady progress over the ice, together with the paws of the dogs on that surface – the clicking of their toenails. But as we came into the narrowest part of the strait the ice was more often mashed up, squeezed together by the wind and water currents. We'd find ourselves in a labyrinth of ice blocks; some of these were the size of cars. The ice would be grinding together; the whole landscape seemed to be groaning at times. As if this wasn't disturbing enough, we were in the hunting grounds of polar bears and wolves. Although polar bears were the more obvious danger, being formidable and almost fearless predators, wolves – though they wouldn't attack a sledge team – certainly could spook the dogs and that might be enough to kill us all, if they lost their nerve and tried to run for home. But the greatest threat out here was simply the water because, at any moment, we might all drop through thin ice and that would be the end of us.

But I was excited despite the fact that no one in the world knew exactly where I was. No one had been known to have crossed the Bering Strait alone – although of course in the days before the cold war, Chukchis and Inuit must have gone back and forth, trading between the two continents. In modern times, though, this would be a unique achievement and I was already proud of what we'd accomplished so far.

I found myself in an even more confusing jumble of broken-up ice. I had to weave my way through clearer corridors between pressure ridges where the ice had crunched together and risen up. It was very slow going, a question of me jumping off and on the sledge to give the dogs a hand, which is not easy when you are wearing a traditional Chukchi reindeer-skin outfit that weighs 15 kg.

But we were making progress. We were working well together and it gave me such pleasure to see how each dog put his heart into the work and obeyed me unquestioningly. I suppose we all knew that we were in danger now; we had to get this right.

That first night a pack of wolves prowled around our camp, no doubt hoping for some of the raw walrus meat. I fired a distress flare to scare them off but soon they were back again, waiting for their chance.

My fear was that my dogs would lose their nerve and run off. Although the truth is that wolves survive by avoiding man and were no serious threat, this didn't stop the dogs from being scared. In the end my sledge dogs decided not to run but to throw their lot in with me. They tried desperately to get into my tent! I'm not sure how they thought I was going to fight off a wolf pack but it was a touching moment. My dogs were going to stick by me, it seemed, no matter what.

We continued on very early the next day. There was little time for sleep; our lives depended on getting off this unstable ice. Besides, I was navigating by compass, taking bearings off the fast-disappearing peninsular behind us. My priority was to press on. We were well into spring and at any moment the ice might start to break up, drowning us all out there. But we were making stunning progress, far greater than I could possibly have hoped.

Now we came to what I felt was the halfway point; the point of no return. Time to stop, stake the dogs out on the ice, find a high point and assess whether I should push on to Alaska or retreat. America must be some twenty-five miles away now, I thought, but I mustn't be tempted into the wrong decision. I didn't even have a gun to defend myself against polar bears, just sacks of raw walrus that I'd fling near any bear that began taking an interest. But this was the least of my concerns; polar bears might be the greatest of all mammal predators but right now I needed to get back onto solid ground.

So I left the dogs and walked forward, counting each step. After 200 paces I found a decent vantage point and began scanning the horizon – east, towards Alaska.

Very soon the wind began to pick up. It was swirling the loose snow around. Nothing unusual in that, but it got worse and I decided to duck down and let it pass. After fifteen or so minutes the wind was dying down. I stood up and discovered that my tracks had been wiped out. There was no need to panic – the dogs were only 200 paces away after all. So I carefully marked my present position by making a flag out of my wind smock, then I began radiating around at a distance of two hundred paces, backwards and forwards. Sooner or later I was bound to come across the dogs.

But I began to get worried. The icescape around me was a labyrinth, a bewildering array of broken white and blue surfaces. Finding the dogs should still be easy – after all, I knew roughly where I'd come from and regardless of having to negotiate this white maze the dogs must be only a few metres from me. Yet there was nothing.

The temperature was dropping fast and soon the wind would pick up again. I worked as hard as I could, but I was perspiring a lot now – that 15 kilo reindeer suit! Of course in sub-zero temperatures you can't just take a swig of water. I pressed on, feeling more and more dehydrated, the dry Arctic air sucking the warmth and moisture out of me. I noticed the sweat on my face was starting to freeze, fixing itself on me like a mask. Things were rapidly getting out of control.

I made myself stop. In these moments of crisis, it's vital not to let events run away – you have to take back control. I knew the next decisions I made could save my life, or kill me. The best thing to do was to duck down behind some ice and get out my emergency stove. I'd rehydrate myself, warm up and then I would be able to think.

I can still remember the sense of relief when the stove lit. 'This is the difference between life and death,' I thought to myself.

Then the stove went out. Strange, but I remained calm. There was certainly no need to panic, at least not yet. I took it apart, cleaned, reassembled and relit it. Again, the stove went out.

It wasn't long before I found the root of the problem. The petrol had somehow become contaminated with oil.

I began thinking through the situation. I must now find a way of getting through the night and, if I managed that, at first light I had to somehow summon the energy to re-start the search for my dogs. If I didn't find them immediately, then – to be realistic – I wouldn't stand a chance. But there was no point of thinking about that, yet. First things first; I had to get through the night.

This meant staying awake. Already I felt like curling up and closing my eyes. The thought of taking a rest, just a little nap, was now almost irresistible. But tonight temperatures were likely to dip to minus thirty with the wind chill effect, even this late in the year – May. I had to fight off any temptation to rest. I had to make myself stand up, pace about. Somehow, I had to keep awake.

Back and forwards I walked, occasionally scooping up a handful of snow to melt in my mouth for moisture but not too much, because that would lower my core body temperature. Back and forwards, back and forwards…

What kept me going was the thought that I had let my dogs down – they'd trusted me to deliver them safely out of here and now I'd messed things up. Or had I? The other thought that had haunted me through the night was that the dogs might have let me down, abandoning me out here. I had done an exhaustive search; they really did seem to have vanished. Perhaps they had lost their nerve after picking up the scent of wolves or a bear. Or maybe they'd just decided they would be better off without me.

I paced about with these nagging thoughts, hour after hour, just waiting for the sun to come up, all the time windmilling, which is pounding my arms against my chest to keep my blood circulation up. Meanwhile, I was also flexing my toes and fingers, fending off frostbite. All the while my mind was whispering seductively, 'Come on, Benedict, just sit down and have a little rest.' This is the voice you have to keep fighting; the voice that leads you to death. You have to keep believing that your body is strong because in survival situations belief is everything. Humans are physically very frail – even the strongest person on the planet would last only a few seconds with a hungry lion or polar bear. But one thing we have which raises us above all other animals is our extraordinary ability to believe in creating our own destiny. We make plans, each and every day – that's what keeps us going. We have purpose; we can envisage a brighter future and hope that tomorrow will be a better day.

The night seemed very long indeed. I began reflecting on why on earth I was out here in the Arctic and bothering to do something as pointless as crossing the Bering Strait. I'd always said that exploration should be about furthering knowledge, not about planting flags or going somewhere in order to conquer things and make your mark. Essentially this particular expedition had always been about learning skills from the Chukchis and how they lived out here with the help of their dogs. So what should count in the end for me was my dog team, the animals out here on the ice somewhere, characters that were now more like team-mates than dogs. Together we'd found a way of crossing the Arctic wilderness.

The night went on and I grew weaker and stiffer as the cold set in. Although I didn't allow myself to think about the prospect of dying, I thought about how people start praying in these dire circumstances. Even people who don't believe in God suddenly find themselves calling for salvation. I couldn't do that – the last thing I thought it was sensible to do was start praying to something that I didn't know was actually there. Yet that night I did make a sort of contract and maybe it was a type of prayer to something I could believe in, my dogs. I promised my dog team – aloud, I think – that if I found them I'd immediately head home. I wouldn't carry on to Alaska, but abandon my ambitions and instead get them safely back.

Was I in fact praying to a higher power? I don't know. But my promise that night definitely made me feel better as I walked up and down on the ice. I knew that if I pulled through then I'd be doing the right thing by not further risking the lives of those ten dogs.

First light came. I saw, almost immediately, the worst possible sight. I climbed up onto a nearby chunk of ice and looked around. I knew exactly where I was; I identified precisely where I had left the dogs… and they were not there.

Now I knew I was alone, and that thought seemed to be worse than the realisation that I was going to die out here in the Arctic. All I cared about was that I was standing absolutely alone amongst melting pack ice. My body, my clothes, my dog team, in fact my entire expedition would disappear forever once the ice had melted. There'd be no funeral; no one would even know what had happened to me.

But then I became aware of a faint smell; a strange odour of something like rotting meat. I wondered if there was a dead animal nearby. Then I smiled, because I knew it could only be walrus meat. I was downwind of my sledge, and the breath of my ten dogs.

I found them only twenty metres away, hidden behind a shelf of ice. Soon I was down on my hands and knees, hugging all the dogs while they nuzzled me. We had a bit of a feast of raw walrus, which I ate with them, and soon I was brewing tea with my main stove.

I then fulfilled my promise, turning the sled around. You should have seen the face of Top Dog when he realised we were heading home. For a second he wasn't sure, and then suddenly the realisation struck and all the dogs were bouncing about, expressing gratitude, joy and relief!

We weren't safe yet, though. We worked day and night; the dogs following their scent trail back across the ice and finally onto firm ground. Three months ago this place, a barren, treeless land capped with snow that was pounded hard by a relentless wind, had been a death zone to me. But it says something about how much I had grown during the experience as the pitiless tundra was something I now saw as safety. I had two of the best days of my life as we sped our way home over the white, seemingly infinite expanse.

This is what exploration was about for me. I was no longer thinking in terms of survival; thanks to the dogs who'd put their trust in me, I had come to see a seemingly hostile environment as somewhere more like home. This was fundamental to all my expeditions – being able to report back with not just an outsider's perspective but understanding something of what it was like for the local people, the Chukchis and others.

In the end it had to be a joint effort. The dogs had the strength, physique and experience to negotiate the hazards of the Arctic and I had what all humans have: an ability to strategise and an ability – indeed a need – to believe in something. Part of that belief is in ourselves; our ability to effect change, but in order to keep going it seems that we also have to believe in something beyond ourselves – our plans, our loved ones and, for some perhaps, God.

This seems to be true whether you are fighting for survival or just struggling along in everyday life – having to hold down a job, revising for exams or triumphantly striving for greatness. Belief in something is what enables us to get out of bed every day. It seems to me to be about more than food, where the next meal is coming from. With only that to think about, people seem to fade away. Rather, it's about what we are going to do with the day, what we might achieve and what we might fashion out of tomorrow.

# IAN COLQUHOUN...

## ... ON LOSING HIS LEGS IN AN HORRIFIC ASSAULT

*'I thought it would have been better if I had just been left to burn. These feelings, though perfectly natural, didn't last long and I soon realised those who had signed the forms had no choice. After a couple of days I began to understand and my attitude changed. I had a choice. Lie in my bed crying about it forever, or just do my best and get on with it. I chose the latter.'*

In August 2002 I moved from Scotland to Dundalk in the Irish Republic to start anew. I was twenty-four at the time and needed to escape the drink and drugs lifestyle I had succumbed to in Scotland. I missed my friends, my family and my team: the beloved Hibernian FC (Hibs). In spite of this, things were going well; I was working two jobs, I loved the town and the people.

But then on Christmas morning 2002, for no apparent reason, I became the victim of a hideous, unprovoked and violent attack after a Christmas Eve party at the home of a girl I had been seeing for a mere ten days. I was beaten unconscious by two, possibly three people, and the attackers, assuming I was dead, set the house alight to hide their crime. They sabotaged the smoke alarm and jammed the doors shut so that, if I did regain consciousness, I would be unable to escape. I was going to die. Until one heroic member of the local Garda (police) braved the blazing inferno to get me out.

After the attack, I discovered that all of my personal possessions, including my wallet, mobile phone and a new, expensive designer jacket, had been stolen. I was then taken to the burns unit in Dublin's St James's Hospital. My family and friends were informed by telephone, and through Scottish police, that I was going to die. They made their way to Dublin.

I had dropped into a coma and didn't wake until some seven weeks later. I had full thickness burns to my chest, abdomen, parts of my arms and, worst of all, to my legs. I had complete renal failure, my lungs were full of black liquid and my heart was failing. I also had minor burns to my upper arms, chin, hands and a nasty head wound, consistent with the assault.

My legs had to be amputated because they were so badly burned. All that was left was bone, and gangrene would have been a serious risk had they not been removed, although amputation by no means guaranteed my survival. I even contracted a rare Asian strain of the MRSA superbug whilst in hospital.

I remember things about the coma; some were to do with my surroundings and would have a simple explanation, but other aspects were of a spiritual or even supernatural nature and can never be explained.

One of the side effects of the drugs given to people in comas is that when they wake up they often hallucinate or say strange things. I made lots of suggestive comments to the nurses that I was later embarrassed about, but I suppose they had heard it all before; they were lovely to me.

While I was in the coma, fighting for my life, thousands of people all over the world were praying for me. When I eventually regained full consciousness, it was left to my mum and sister to explain what had happened. At first I didn't believe them and, believe it or not, I actually thought I should be signing myself out as I had work to go to. I asked for a pair of crutches so that I could go home. It simply hadn't sunk in.

When I saw the injuries, when I eventually had the strength to lift my head, I cried and wailed like a child. Human beings are genetically programmed to be able to cope with the loss of a loved one but the loss of one's legs is something the mind simply isn't designed to deal with. That night, when my visitors went home, I just wanted to kill myself. As I didn't have the strength, and was still under twenty-four-hour observation, it was impossible.

At first I hated my friends and family for signing the forms and allowing the doctors to take my legs away. I thought it would have been better if I had just been left to burn. These feelings, though perfectly natural, didn't last long and I soon realised those who had signed the forms had no choice. After a couple of days I began to understand and my attitude changed. I had a choice. Lie in my bed crying about it forever, or just do my best and get on with it. I chose the latter.

As soon as consultants told me I would be able to get prosthetic legs my mood improved even more, and within three or four days of realising I had lost my legs I was cracking jokes with the nurses and visitors. The biggest concern when I woke from the coma, amazingly, wasn't my legs but whether or not I would be able to have sex again. Although I still couldn't move, I soon realised there was nothing wrong in that department when a sexy pop video, 'All the Things She Said' by t.A.T.u, was played on the hospital television. That made me realise everything was still in working order in that respect. My face, bottom, back, genitals, neck and head, thankfully, weren't burnt at all.

Everyone agreed that the best place for me, once I was fit enough, was back home in Scotland. Including amputations and skin grafts, I had had fifteen operations, but I still needed two major ones; one to replace the black, crusty, burnt skin on my chest and abdomen and another far more serious one to cover a huge patch of exposed bone below my one remaining knee. My left leg is amputated above the knee and the right just below.

On 18 February 2003 the Irish Air Force flew me home to Scotland. I was admitted to the burns unit at St John's Hospital in my home town, Livingston, where I was to have those final two operations and, from there, rebuild my life.

It was a relief to get back to Scotland, not just because I knew someone had tried to kill me in Ireland but also because visitors flooded in. Everyone who loved and cared about me came to visit.

I spent just over two months at St John's where the plastics team worked wonders completing my surgery. The low point during that time was when a surgeon said just before that all important knee operation, 'If this operation isn't successful, you'll be in a wheelchair for the rest of your life.'

Thankfully, the eleven-hour operation was a success. Surgeons covered the exposed bone below my knee with a bit of muscle taken from my left forearm and 'plumbed it in' with an artery from my arm, meaning it could get a blood supply. This procedure is called a bi-scapular flap. Other operations in

St John's were also great successes, though the daily dressing changes were agony.

That April, I was moved to Astley Ainslie Rehabilitation Hospital in order to be fitted with prosthetic limbs. At first I loved it there; it was great compared to being confined to a single room in St John's for so long. Although I was fitted with prosthetics, a combination of MRSA, my wounds taking too long to heal and the development of a bone disease in my knee called osteomyelitis meant that I was discharged from hospital in October 2003 without prosthetic limbs. During my time in Astley Ainslie I had been rushed back to St John's for a further small amputation because of the osteomyelitis, though fortunately the surgery and long-term antibiotics eradicated this problem.

I spent the next fifteen months in a wheelchair, waiting to be re-admitted to hospital to undergo the last operation so that I would finally be able to wear prosthetic legs. I wasn't allowed back into St John's because of the MRSA issue, though by then I was rid of the infection.

I needed to do something; I was going crazy. Despite moving into a nice house in Edinburgh when I got out of hospital, I was bored and I needed something to focus my mind on. I had put on a lot of weight having not walked for so long, so I started going to my local gym and doing upper-body work. I also started attending university on a part-time basis studying military history, one of my pet topics. It was on these courses that my potential to be a writer and historian was again spotted.

I had a bad accident in 2004 at Hampden Park when my team lost a cup final to Livingston. I was catapulted from my wheelchair after the wheels struck TV cables that shouldn't have been where they were and, to make matters worse, I landed on the stump that needed the last operation. Still this did not speed up my return to hospital, though the severity of the wound meant I now needed drastic orthopaedic surgery rather than a simple skin graft. I eventually had the operation in February 2005 but I was in constant pain from the accident at Hampden Park until well after the last surgery.

The low point of the limbo period, between being discharged from hospital in late 2003 and getting the operation in early 2005, was when I returned to Hibs' home ground, Easter Road. I had previously been at home on the east stand with the more hard core and vocal element of the Hibs' supporters. When I returned though, I had to go in the wheelchair section of the main stand as there was no wheelchair access on the east stand. It was great to be back at Easter Road but the atmosphere in the main stand was awful; there was no singing. It was more like a library. I longed to get my new legs and get back on the east stand where I belonged.

My final operation in February 2005 was a complete success and, once the stitches were out, I was back at Astley Ainslie Hospital that summer. It was hard work doing the rehab, especially as the muscles I had used to stand and walk hadn't been used in two and a half years. And with determination and some fantastic help from my physiotherapists slowly, but surely, I learned to walk again – firstly parallel bars, then with a walking frame and finally with crutches.

It was an amazing feeling to be walking again. I had feared that because my stumps were skin grafted they wouldn't be strong enough to take my prosthetic legs but the more I walked, the easier it got. When the physios showed me how to tackle stairs, which I managed successfully, I was elated as I knew I would be able to get back on the east stand in time for the new season. It was great being back on that stand, especially when we beat a hitherto undefeated Hearts two–nil. The atmosphere on the east stand was amazing; I was so glad to be back.

Now I walk with a fixed knee on my left side, and I have a suction held leg on my right with a Hibs' badge laminated into the socket! In 2004 I learned to drive using hand controls and I now own an adapted car. Alan Drysdale of Edinburgh did the adaptations. I continued studying part-time until May 2006 and then I did a couple of newspaper and magazine articles to get some much-needed cash.

A good year for me was 2006. I appeared on a science programme called *Men in White*, where the science team made me an attachment for my leg that included an iPod, disco lights, an alarm and a pedometer. Through the lovely producer of this show I was also taken on by a specialist agency 'Amputees in Action', who supply amputees to TV and film to add that extra bit of realism to action scenes.

Then in August I got a publishing deal from Mirage Books to release my autobiography, *Burnt*, and getting that deal has opened the door to a number of other literary projects. I have since written a series of historical novels and am writing a number of books for charity. I hope to continue writing long-term, both as an author and as a freelance journalist.

My scars are fading and in early 2007 Amputees in Action got me my first film role, playing a badly wounded sailor in a film called *Ocean of Fear* filmed at Pinewood Studios in Buckinghamshire. That was one of the most amazing experiences of my life; I had a spoken part and performed a dangerous underwater stunt.

Although I have been through a terrible ordeal, my life is now strangely better though, of course I miss my legs, dancing and playing football.

I have finally started using my real talent – writing – and other problems from my past, such as issues I used to have with my family, with drink and drugs are now completely sorted. My only other worry was that women wouldn't find me attractive but I've long since realised that simply is not the case. My amputations haven't ruined my sex life, although my experience in Ireland has taught me to be a bit more wary about whom I choose to see. I'm not bitter about my physical condition. Now people see me for who I am and if they have a problem with that then they're not worth knowing.

I stopped listening to dance music after losing my legs but I have rediscovered my love for it. I am super-fit and the 'man boobs' I developed whilst in hospital are now solid pecks, with muscular arms and shoulders. I still go to the gym every day and I'm a lot more health conscious than when I was a 'drunken waster' back in Livingston.

I suffered some phantom limb pain after the amputations, usually when I was stressed, but I rarely get any nowadays. My biggest inspiration in my recovery, apart from visits from Olivia Giles, a quadruple amputee, and Hibs' striker Mixu Paatelainen, has been my friends and family, who are simply brilliant.

My hopes for the future are now a lot clearer than they have ever been. Keep writing, keep walking and avoid any illnesses that may hamper my future mobility. I also hope to continue my acting and stunt work and undertake voluntary stints lecturing to physiotherapy students at Edinburgh's Queen Margaret University College. I would also love to settle down and have a family but I have a lot of lost time to make up for. I would like to go back and get a PhD to do with the Jacobite War and I also want a crack at the TV show *Mastermind*.

As for my future fears, I do worry about losing my knee and the mobility problems that would cause. I am also afraid that further books I write may be rejected but that is a fear shared by all authors.

If asked to judge the quality of the medical care that I received, I would give it ten out of ten. Despite my problems before moving to Ireland, the unprovoked attempt on my life and all the pain and suffering I have endured, through amputation and painful burns treatment, I am probably happier now than I have ever been. This is a tribute not only to courage and determination but to the human spirit and desire to live that is in all of us, if we choose to look hard enough.

# KERRI-ANN CARTWRIGHT...

## ... ON WINNING £2.5 MILLION ON THE NATIONAL LOTTERY

'By the time I had arrived at the shop they already knew that there was only one winning ticket and it was for just over £2.5 million. When they told me, I was even more stunned. It didn't feel real; I thought I was dreaming. We checked the ticket once more against the Internet and it was at that point I knew for a fact that it was the winner.'

It was January 2007, I was twenty-seven years old and Christmas had just passed. The new college term had begun and my three-year-old daughter was back in her nursery routine. I was a mature student and working part-time in the bar at a local golf club, which I really enjoyed. Being a single parent, there wasn't a lot of spare money for luxuries but my life was good and, on the whole, I was happy. I had a long-term outlook; I was trying to set myself up with a new career for when my daughter was older.

One night in mid January I went to bed as normal and had a dream that I had won the lottery. I didn't see the numbers but it was all about me after having just won. The feeling I had was so vivid and it felt so real. Even in the morning after I had woken I still felt as if I had actually won and that I was still dreaming. It took me a few minutes to gather myself together and get on with the daily routine. I had to tell myself that it was just a dream; it wasn't real.

I was at work later that day and I mentioned my dream to my manager and the usual conversation came up. What would I do if I won for real? Then I was told in a jovial manner to get back to work and stop dreaming.

It was Tuesday 23 January and my daughter had been really good. She asked for a drink of blackcurrant at bedtime. We didn't have any as it wasn't a drink that I often bought but I promised her I would buy some the following day and she went to bed happy. The next day was another college day and that lunchtime I ran to the local Tesco store to fulfil my promise. I picked up the bottle of blackcurrant and noticed that it was on offer so I decided to get two bottles. I went through the checkout and as I was leaving I passed the lottery counter by the door. With the change in my hand I queued and filled out my line of usual numbers; as I handed over my slip I also asked for an extra lucky dip, which I didn't often do. I put the ticket in my purse and went back to college.

That evening the cable TV network wasn't working at home so I got my head down, did some assignment work and listened to music. It was after 10 p.m. when I decided to get ready for bed. I went upstairs, got into bed and switched on the TV; it had a free-standing aerial. I wanted to see if I could catch the end of the news but instead the lottery programme was on and I remembered buying a ticket earlier that day. I watched the balls roll out of the machine and realised that I had left my ticket in my purse downstairs. I took my phone and saved the numbers on a text message to check in the morning. I typed them into the phone in the order they came out of the machine. Shortly after, I switched the TV off and went to sleep.

The next morning was like any other. I got my daughter ready for nursery and myself ready for college. It was the morning break and I went down to the college canteen for the usual snack. My friend Jo decided that she wasn't going that morning so I went with some other people from my course. I was at the till when I remembered that my ticket was in my purse. I sat down and pulled out my ticket. I checked the numbers and was thrilled to see I had won £10 with three numbers. Then I saw the fourth match and said to a friend I had got four numbers. It was then I saw the fifth and I just stood up. 'Oh my God,' I remembered saying as I started heading back to the classroom to get my bag. I was off to Tesco to claim what I thought was about a thousand pounds with my five numbers.

I entered the classroom and saw Jo. I simply said 'I've won the lottery, I've got five numbers.' She didn't really believe me so I handed her the ticket and my phone as I explained that I had typed the numbers in the night before. She thought it was another of my wind-ups. Jo started to double-check the numbers and smiled as she said, 'You've probably just put these in your phone.'

As my excitement grew Jo started to check them on the web and I began to gather my things together. A few minutes passed while she checked the numbers. 'Oh my God! You've really won!' she exclaimed.

'I know,' I replied.

Then I looked at her. She was turning a funny pale shade. She simply said, 'No, you've won, really won.' It still didn't really sink in until she said I had all six numbers. The room fell silent for a few seconds and I felt my legs go numb. There were a few people on the other side of the class who came over to see what the commotion was as Jo handed me the unsigned ticket.

After that I can remember packing my things, leaving college and thinking, 'Stay calm. Just get your things and go.' I wasn't even sure if I was floating or walking. I got to the entrance lobby and then headed for my car. I was trying to stay calm and composed but steadily paranoia started to kick in and my walking became a steady jog across the car park.

I struggled my way into the car and, after throwing my bags on the back seat, I locked the door behind me. I picked my phone up to call my mum – it was engaged. I tried her mobile but there was no answer there, either... this was incredibly frustrating. I swore as I threw my phone on the passenger seat and cried, 'Just answer the phone!'

I was still in shock; I didn't know what to do first. I started reversing out of the parking space and just stopped halfway out. I had to speak to my mum. I called again and, this time, she answered. I could hardly speak at that point and just cried; at first she thought there was something wrong with my daughter. Eventually I struggled to find my words. She screamed and shouted the news out to my aunty who works with her in their bridal shop.

At first I couldn't remember the journey to the shop but managed to get myself there, despite my shock. I just pulled up outside, stopping in the middle of the road and they both ran out. Mum parked the car for me and I went inside. By the time I had arrived at the shop, they already knew that there was only one winning ticket and it was for just over £2.5 million. When they told me, I was even more stunned. It didn't feel real; I thought I was dreaming. We checked the ticket once more against the Internet and it was at that point I knew for a fact that it was the winner.

We made the all-important phone call to Camelot, answered a few questions and I was told to sign the ticket, keep it safe and wait for a call back. Word quickly spread through the immediate family and they all started to gather in the shop, which had already been closed for the day. I decided to go and get my daughter from the nursery early and told everyone to go up to the golf club where I worked to celebrate. I knew being midweek in January the place would be deserted. I quickly dragged my boss to one side and broke the good news. I then told him that I was unable to work that night. The celebrations started from then.

I called my dad to tell him the news, then my best friend Dawn. I didn't say straight out that I had won the lottery I just told her the figure and we just screamed. It suddenly went dead and I realised that I had run out of credit on my pay-as-you-go phone. I had to top it up and then explain to her that I had run out of money... it seems ironic but was very funny at the time. Later that day a lovely lady from Camelot came to chat with me. We discussed the arrangements for the following day and she asked how much of an advance I wanted. I was still in a daze and replied, 'Enough for the taxi home.'

At home that night I couldn't sleep at all. I had gone to bed but just couldn't switch off so ended up in front of the fire with a hot drink at 4 a.m. By 8 a.m. we were on our way to the Camelot office to verify the win and collect the cheque. That whole day was fantastic and one that I will never forget. I remember holding my breath as they took the ticket to be verified through their machine; it was rejected at first so each number was typed in separately. Eventually it was verified... that was the longest two minutes ever.

The press conference followed and I can remember a sea of photographers and journalists in the room. The whole day was amazing from start to finish. I took the view that if this was my five minutes of fame then I was going to enjoy every second of it.

Since then life hasn't been the same, although I have kept my feet firmly on the ground. I think having a young child has helped me keep perspective in my life. The biggest difference for me is the ability to live a financially stress-free life and the security of knowing that my family will be OK. I still enjoy being a mum most of all and having more time to spend with her and watching her grow is amazing. She has continued to be the focus of my life.

I have had so many more experiences and opportunities since the win, such as radio interviews, photo shoots, charity events and presentations. I have met lots of amazing people and made lots of great friends. I have also been able to spend money on luxury cars, houses and holidays; things that without the win I would never have been able to afford. To complete everything I have met an amazing man who I hope will be my 'happy ever after'.

# DAVE HEELEY...

## ... ON RUNNING SEVEN MARATHONS, IN SEVEN DAYS, ON SEVEN CONTINENTS, DESPITE BEING BLIND

*'The finishing line in London held so many positives. It was simply an incredible ending. We had done it. We had run ourselves into the history books; I was the first blind person in the world to run seven marathons, on seven continents, in seven days. It was such an emotional moment and is something I will never, ever forget.'*

I was diagnosed at a very early age with a disease called retinitis pigmentosa (RP). The disease is a progressive illness of the retina and, essentially, it meant that I was going to go blind. RP has all sorts of stages and when it was first discovered that I had the condition, I had night blindness but I wasn't 'blind'. I had very poor vision; I was extremely short-sighted, but I insisted that I went through mainstream schools regardless of my sight problems. I had difficulty reading the blackboard and seeing in dimly lit places but I could still get by – I could still see enough. As a kid I never truly understood the diagnosis myself and the technology that we have today was not available. At ten years of age, when someone says that you are going blind and you can still see a football 200 yards down the pitch you think, 'Well really? Am I?' Up until the age of ten, because I thought I saw what everyone else saw, I was known as a bit of a clumsy kid. I just imagined that everyone else went through the same thing, so I never actually questioned it too much. My little brain couldn't register the fact that I was going to lose my sight.

I always say that I don't profess to understand RP, because I don't want to know what causes it; I want the cure. It's not that I don't care; I do, but I am more interested in the solutions than I am in the details. It is a strange disease that can strike at any time. You can get people who are born with it, or people who contract it at ten, twelve, twenty, forty; whenever. There are many different strains of the illness and people are affected by it in various ways. In my strain the male is the sufferer and the female is the carrier, so it came through my mum's genes. My granddad was blind; he had the same problem as I do. Fortunately in our family I am the only one who actually has it, so hopefully the strain has skipped a generation or two. As there are so many variations of the disease, I can only speak for myself and my experience of it. I was well into my thirties before my sight went completely. Even now I still have a light differential threshold – I am not 100 per cent blind. I was told that by the age of thirty-five I would be completely blind; I am now fifty-one, so I am certainly living on some fantastic borrowed time. Only four per cent of people classed as 'blind' are actually totally blind. It is a comfort barrier for me, because I can still tell the difference between night and day. In the same way a child might go to bed with a particular blanket, knowing that I am not yet fully in the world of the dark is a bloody big comfort to me.

Progressive blindness is hard to describe. A good way to explain it is: on Monday I looked across the street and saw a house. On the Tuesday I looked across the street and saw the hedgerow. On the Wednesday I saw the curb on the other side of the road and on Thursday I was seeing the white line on the street. On Friday I start thinking, 'Hang on a minute, where's the gutter gone?' Obviously it wasn't over a single week; it didn't happen that quickly, but it was like that, just progressively over many years. I suddenly started realising things, 'Last year I could see the tree at the bottom of the garden – where's it gone?' It sounds strange but until you start looking for things that you would normally see, you don't really notice. It is only when you glance and think, 'Oh bloody hell, I can't see the kettle any more,' that it hits you.

I have always kept myself busy rather than sitting on a chair in the garden looking at a wall waiting for the day when I couldn't see it any more. Over the last thirty years I haven't given myself a chance to worry about it. Even as a youngster I was always active and I played a lot of sport. Sadly though, it got to the point, when I was around sixteen, where I couldn't see the football any more. I couldn't see a cricket ball to be able to play that, and tennis or other sports that required eyesight also became impossible. My sight really started nose-diving around that time.

My two ambitions when I left school were to drive and join the military. My dad and I had planned to invest in a car together. I sought a career in the military; I wanted to join the army and I wanted, ultimately, to be in the SAS. Sadly, the realisation really hit me around the age of seventeen – I was going blind. All my friends were taking driving lessons and

I was told that I would never drive. Even now, if I am going to do something, until I actually get it point blank that the answer is no, I will pursue it. To the point where I even went for the army medical and at the end thought I had actually got through. But I was exempt because of my sight. So my only two ambitions, driving a car and a career in the military, had disappeared. I was gutted.

I got an office-based job fairly quickly after school. My sight was obviously changing my life dramatically; everything I had wanted to do was now impossible. Early on in my life this had caused me a great deal of stress and worry. I went through years on my own feeling sorry for myself. When I got to about twenty-two/twenty-three, I was just going through a divorce and I had been made redundant. I sat there and thought, 'Christ, why me?' It was around that time I changed my viewpoint on my entire life. I felt that if the good book says we've got 'three score and ten' then I've got a hell of a lot of years left to be feeling sorry for myself. I knew that moping around was not the way forward. For me it was a case of not worrying about what I can't do, but concentrating on the things I *can* do. I perked myself up and started looking on the positive side. Even though I would often sit behind my desk daydreaming about travelling the world and the possibilities in the military, I knew I couldn't do that. So I made the best of what I had and of what I could do. It was then that my life transformed – this wasn't going to hold me back.

I have done a few different jobs in my time. I had a good run in the building industry. I got made redundant, though, and after spending a little bit of time as a 'jack the lad', trading here and there where I could, I set up my own business. We were selling and distributing suspended ceilings partitions. I had a partner and we ran the company for the best part of nine years. But sadly the building industry is always the first to feel the pressure in tough financial times and when the recession hit us in the 1990s we got collared for an awful lot of bad debt so the company folded.

It was tricky during this period because when you're over forty nobody wants you. Over forty and *blind*; you haven't got a prayer. I was offered work but I found most of it a bit uninspiring. Packing boxes in a factory was a bit below my skill base. So, again, I changed my tactics a little bit and I ended up going back to college for three years in Birmingham. I did craft and design, carpentry skills, wood turning, upgraded my brail and I learned IT skills. I love to design things in my head and I love to start making them. I love the feel and smell of wood. I could lose myself for days – for weeks – in my workshop.

Around then I got a guide dog for the first time. I couldn't believe how much it actually enhanced my life. It gave me independence and freedom. I decided then that I would raise as much awareness and funding for Guide Dogs for the Blind as a thank you for what they had given me. I became one of the top fundraisers and volunteers for Guide Dogs. I managed to build a great network of fundraising contacts. Later these would come in handy.

At school I loved running. At secondary school my claim to fame was holding the 1,500 m record for five years on the trot. Sadly, when I got to the age of sixteen my sight was so bad that it became difficult for me to run on my own. I had to give up track and cross-country running. Guide runners were not really around then – they are still not that well known now – so I gave it up. I went more than twenty years without running. A great friend who I had known for many years, Joe Whitehouse, effectively became my first guide runner. I realised it was still in me, I still enjoyed it and I haven't looked back since. Joe ran with me in my first two London Marathons but sadly in the second, at eight miles, he picked up an injury. I found out later that he refused to let me down and ran with me until the end, causing him tremendous pain.

Running for me is a sport that I thoroughly enjoy. There are challenges to it, it keeps you fit and if I can use it to inspire someone along the way then I am happy. I ran the London Marathon in 2002, and have done every year since. Malcolm Carr, aka Mac, who I met through the West Bromwich Harriers Running Club many years ago, took over as my guide runner following Joe's injury. The partnership I have with Mac, and with any guide runner, is one built on trust. We are tied at the wrist by a cord, which is approximately 18 inches long, and I can follow his body movements – so if he suddenly goes one way I go with him. I've had no really bad accidents to date, touch wood. So somewhere along the line the partnership is working quite well.

Running marathons was great but I had always been looking for something to do that was a bit different. A year after my first marathon, I was in my workshop listening to the radio. Sir Ranulph Fiennes came on to talk about completing the seven marathons, seven continents, in seven days challenge. He was the first able-bodied person to run the seven-marathon challenge. It sounded fantastic and I thought it would be a great vehicle for raising awareness and funds if I could be the first blind person to do it. That set the scene for the whole thing. I wondered if I could do it – of course I could. And that was it; the ultimate challenge was set.

It took five years to organise and it took me around six months to actually convince Mac. I knew the training would be serious but I didn't really know where we should go from there. So we continued the normal marathon training from the London Marathon until we acquired a physiotherapist to help us. We managed to get Dr Philip Glasgow, from the Sports Institute in Northern Ireland, on board. He topped and tailed us and then started putting the training schedule together.

'This is literally a blind schedule for a blind runner. I haven't got a clue,' he said. He explained that he could put together a marathon schedule to run a marathon fast, or to run a marathon slow. But nobody has ever put a training programme together to run seven marathons, not only in a row but also on seven different continents – taking climate, humidity, temperature, time zones etc. into account. That is without even considering the logistics of the project: sleeping, eating, flights and other factors which would have a significant effect on our bodies. Where do we start? We got going and over a period of six months, with the information I was feeding back to him, he was able build a training schedule, and, testament to it, we completed the challenge.

In the UK I was supporting Guide Dogs for the Blind, and around the world I was supporting other blind-associated charities. I wrote to a lot of people to get funding. I also made friends with a chap from London called Dave English, who runs the Bunbury Celebrity Cricket Team, and Dave passed me onto a couple of his sponsors. Lucozade supplied all the supplements we used around the world and for the six months training period leading up to the challenge. North Face supplied us with all of our running kit, travel bags, camel packs for drinks and other accessories. Mercedes provided transport in most of the countries we ran in. Our main sponsors Costcutter and some of their allied suppliers supported us financially.

I had planned to support Guide Dogs for the Blind regardless and towards the latter end of planning they agreed to officially come on board about six months before the challenge started. This relieved a lot of the financial pressure as they underwrote all the travel costs. So with all those sponsors the costs were covered and it became a reality. We had to do it.

Organising was tough; describing it as a 'nightmare' would be an understatement. But we knew what we wanted to achieve and we had to start seriously planning. The seven continents were set in stone, because there are only seven continents in the world. The Falklands would be the starting point because it counts as Antarctica but it is obviously on the fringes. Sir Ranulph ran in the Falklands, so if it was good enough for him it was good enough for me. Actually, running in the heart of Antarctica can be extremely tricky. Getting in is fine but you only need an hour or so of bad weather before getting out becomes problematic. So the Falklands would be our starting point. After five years of planning and training we kicked off on 7 April 2008, at a minute past midnight GMT on the Falkland Islands. We started and finished the marathon at Mount Pleasant Air Base, running out of the base and back in on the runway. It was actually the first time that anyone has ever been allowed to run on the runway.

The initial plan was to start on the Falklands (Antarctica), then go to Argentina (South America) to run in Buenos Aires. From there we would go on to Los Angeles (North America), Sydney (Australasia), Singapore (Asia), Cairo (Africa) and finally end with the London Marathon (Europe). But when logistics started to come together, as we were doing the majority of it on scheduled airlines, we had to adjust the plan slightly. It was important to be on single flights. For example from Australia to Singapore it was going to be two flights, so we changed it to Dubai, to cover Asia, which was only one flight. These alterations cut down a lot of time, saving us the hassle of changing planes. Our route plan changed about six or seven times.

Our start time was to be midnight GMT, but it was 8.01 p.m. local time in the Falklands, so we were running at night. We then flew from there in the early hours of the morning in a private Learjet to Rio de Janeiro, Brazil, and we did the second marathon on the Monday, so technically we ran two on the same day. Then we flew from Rio on the Monday evening, got to Los Angeles and ran on the Tuesday. The reason for doing two in one day was that when we flew from Los Angeles on the Tuesday evening we lost Wednesday because of the time zones. So we landed in Australia on the Thursday and did the marathon in Sydney during the day. We ran Dubai the following day, which we started at eight o'clock in the morning, because of the heat. When it came to Africa because of flight times we had to start even earlier, at seven in the morning. Then we got back to London for the Sunday to finish on the London Marathon. This was not only my seventh marathon that week, but it was also my seventh consecutive London Marathon.

The marathons we were running were official routes but they were not official marathons. It would have been impossible to run organised marathons in all these places not least because most are done on Sundays. The routes were organised and mapped with GPS. In the Falklands the military plotted the course and arranged everything, in Rio Philip had to do it. In LA a local athletics club and The Blind Association helped us map the route, same with Sydney. Three ex-pat athletics clubs did Dubai. Tunisia was plotted, but the police there changed the route halfway through, but due to GPS it was still all spot on distance wise. Then obviously the London Marathon was the only official one, with other runners. ITV Central filmed the whole challenge along the way and the thirty-minute documentary they produced was fantastic.

We had a team of me, Mac, Philip and David Gagen (our logistics man). There were also two representatives from Guide Dogs for the Blind – David Newell and Nikki Wright. Eric MacInnes presented the documentary and Kevin Capon filmed it. There were eight of us in total. Also Victoria Cheeseman, who worked for Travel Counsellors, helped us organise all the travelling and slept in her office on a camp bed for the whole week so that she could keep an eye on flight times. There was a lot of room for error so she was a very important part of the team. We had a very tight schedule; once we had finished a marathon it was straight to business – there was no time to relax. Get in that shower, eat this, in the car and we're off to the airport. With sleeping it was simply a case of get it where you can.

The hardest of the marathons was by far Rio, simply because it started eight hours after finishing the Falklands leg; six hours of flying, two hours sorting out airport administration then running another 26.2 miles was tough. Also we had no support on the ground other than our team so it was very lonely, but we completed it nevertheless.

Everywhere else we had fantastic support that really helped drive us. The crowds certainly lifted our spirits and of course London was a fantastic homecoming. Everyone embraced us, friends and especially family were waiting, which was incredible.

In total we ran 183.4 miles, 250,000 steps, all in under 168 hours. We ran fairly consistent times, too. Falklands was 4h 14min. Rio was 4h 45min. LA was 4h 35min. Sydney was 4h 40min. Dubai, which was certainly the hottest, was 4h 55min. Tunisia was 4h 44min. Sadly, London was our slowest because

Mac got totally dehydrated and we had to keep stopping. So our time was 5h 20min. Normally I do a marathon in 3h 30min but we were pacing ourselves. Philip had worked out that we were going to do them on certain heartbeats. He was happy with us basing the pace on 4h 30min for each. We really had no time to beat, just so long as we got them all done in the seven days.

People were pushing for an actual number on the money we raised and a figure of £375,000 was announced about a year ago. The thing is though, what we achieved has left a legacy, hopefully for a long time. We'll never know exactly what it has brought in as the awareness is priceless. Guide Dogs have said that now a lot more people are sponsoring puppies because of the challenge. Lots of money is coming in and it is hard to directly identify where all the money has come from or attribute the reasons; whether or not we are responsible for a lot of it is impossible to say. We'll never know an exact value for what we have done but we know it's a lot.

The coverage we got in the media, on the Internet, in the papers, on television and the radio was hugely positive for the charity as well. The calculations were done and the charity said that to achieve the kind of coverage that we generated would have cost them around £5.5 million. The awareness really is phenomenal.

Completing the challenge catapulted me into a fantastic career. Now I am the Physical Activities Ambassador for my local council, Sandwell – in the heart of the Black Country. I am also the ambassador for the Birmingham Half Marathon. I'm working alongside a couple of PR companies and am doing a lot of motivational talks. I am working within schools where I am hopefully inspiring kids and getting them into sport. I have done talks in Belfast and Holland, among other places; I have been all over the place. The future isn't looking too bad. I am still doing my carpentry and, of course, I am still running. Completing the challenge has certainly raised my profile; when I run now people know whom I am.

The whole thing came together so well and the logistics fell into place wonderfully. I think the challenge was simply meant to be. All the places we visited were incredible. For me these places were obviously not visual but rather it was what I could feel, smell, hear and what I was told. Dubai had a different smell; there was a different texture to the atmosphere because it was so hot. I remember in Tunisia we could smell the fresh air and the sea – it was great. Then obviously in London I could hear the crowds, feel the excitement, smell the city and sense the ambience of what the London Marathon is all about.

There was pain; there is no denying that. We went through the mill a little bit. But looking back on it now I think of it as a whole story, a book – each chapter, each page, each paragraph is just part of the whole thing. The pain was there for a reason.

The finishing line in London held so many positives. It was simply an incredible ending. We had done it. We had run ourselves into the history books; we were the third people in the world to complete this challenge. I was the first blind person in the world to run seven marathons, on seven continents, in seven days. It was such an emotional moment and is something I will never, ever forget. My kids were there at the end in London, which was fabulous. To have my family there at that moment was amazing; it was the icing on the cake.

Once the emotion was out of my head I then knew the awareness that I had just created for blind people around the world and it was an unbelievable feeling.

I truly hope that I have inspired people to set their goals high. If I have just inspired one person, then it has all been worthwhile. The message is whatever you want to do, you can. Don't ever say you can't, because you can. Simple as that; if you want to do it, you can find a way. Every painful step I have gone through, every ice bath I was plunged into, was absolutely worth it, and it gives me such pride to think that somewhere along the line I've helped somebody.

# KELLY GREEN...

## ... ON BEING BITTEN BY A BROWN RECLUSE SPIDER

*'I knew then that the spider had bitten me and that I could be in a lot of trouble. The swelling was disgusting; it looked like a bright red balloon under my skin. It had a purple outline. It looked like something from a bad zombie film. The flesh on my leg was dying, I needed to get to hospital and soon.'*

My brother had been living in the USA for about five years and insisted that I come and visit. I incorporated visiting him with a mini camping adventure with a friend. We were both photography students at the time so we were taking landscape and wildlife pictures in the woods. Colorado is a beautiful state and we were seeing as much as we could of it – the scenery is absolutely stunning.

Anyway, we had been hiking and camping for a few days when I had a nasty fall, which was entirely my fault but resulted in me spraining my ankle. I was gutted as it meant the trip might have to be cut short and I would end up letting my friend down. We set up camp early that night with some

Americans, who we had been hiking with. One of them was medically trained, so she bandaged my ankle up to reduce the swelling. I kept the bandage on all evening, but when I went back to my tent I had to take the dressing off because it was itchy and needed some air.

I had a cooling and numbing muscle-treatment cream on my ankle that my friend had lent me. This kept me numb through the night and helped me sleep. I also took some painkillers, which made me drowsy and gave me a reasonable night.

In the middle of the night, I woke to a strange pain in my leg. I was worried that I may have actually broken my ankle as the sensation was so unusual. So I put the bandage back on as the medically trained girl probably knew best. In the morning I was packing my things up in my tent when I found the most hideous spider that I have ever seen. I didn't know at the time but it was a brown recluse spider. I am not arachnophobic, but I don't like spiders. I can usually get rid of them with a glass and a postcard but I wouldn't touch one out of choice. I had seen spiders out here before but compared with the ones at home in the UK this was particularly disgusting. I shoved it out of my tent and shuddered at the thought of it crawling on me in the night. I didn't once think that it could have bitten me.

I could just walk on my sprained ankle, it was very painful but I pretended to get better. I wanted to stay for another day; I didn't want to let my friend down and head back to my brother's house, cutting the trip short. We carried on that day taking photos and enjoying the breathtaking landscape. My leg was tightly wrapped up in bandages and in my boots so I couldn't see the swelling, but I could certainly feel it.

I was regularly asked if I was OK and I nodded and pretended to be fine – stiff upper lip and all that. But I wasn't all right; my ankle was incredibly painful and it was a weird pain and a particularly overwhelming one. I thought I had a trapped nerve or something that could be causing this horrible sensation.

That evening I was almost in tears from the agony. I had also begun to feel really ill; nauseous from the pain. I had yet to take my boots and bandages off because I knew that when I did the pain would be too severe to put them back on.

That evening one of the American guys spotted a spider and called us all over to look. He said it was a recluse spider and warned us Brits that they are relatively tame, but should be avoided. I had a brief giggle to myself and thought, 'I actually slept with one last night.' I had yet to put two and two together and realise why my ankle was so sore.

I remember asking the guy more about these brown recluse spiders – out of sheer curiosity not because I thought for a moment I may have been bitten. He explained that they can bite, but only when they feel scared or threatened. He told me that sometimes people die from the bites. He even described the pain I had been feeling all day, yet still I didn't put it all together.

I manoeuvred my boot off and, with a great deal of pain, gently removed the bandages. I looked down at my ankle and recoiled in horror at what I saw. I actually remember covering it straight back up again in a very childish display of 'out of sight, out of mind'.

I knew then that the spider had bitten me and that I could be in a lot of trouble. The swelling was disgusting; it looked like a bright red balloon under my skin. It had a purple outline. It looked like something from a bad zombie film. The flesh on my leg was dying, I needed to get to hospital and soon.

I called my friend over and made her look. Then she called everyone else around and made them look. The guy who seemed to be an expert found it to be a hilarious coincidence and enthused at the damage. He was so excited that it had happened, seemingly oblivious to my pain. He liked spiders – the freak!

We knew straight away that it wasn't just damage from walking on a sprained ankle all day because, at the centre of the swelling, was a disgusting-looking spot (a tell-tale sign of a bite). I am quite squeamish when it comes to things like this and the fact that it was my own leg made it a lot worse. I couldn't look at it.

We knew I had to get to hospital so my friend and I, and the American guy who liked the spiders, headed back to the centre. The spider fan even said, without a shred of irony, that I probably shouldn't have left it to fester for twenty-four hours. Duh – I know that now! But he was right; I was fairly stupid to firstly not even notice being bitten and secondly ignore the blatant pain.

I almost didn't get insurance for the trip, which may have made my treatment quite pricey. Luckily I did, and the doctors went straight to work. I was put on a drip and given all sorts of antibiotics. By this time, though, the flesh around the wound looked dead, and sadly it was. It is rare but some people have adverse reactions to the bites and have even been known to lose entire limbs. Often they are just nasty swellings that go down with a bit of cream but occasionally the flesh can die from the toxicity of the venom. The doctor seemed to share the bizarre enthusiasm for the spiders as well – it felt strange that the horrible thing that had done this to me was receiving so much praise.

They did surgery on my leg that involved, in layman's terms, cutting the infected area away and binning it, which was as horrible as it sounds. After the procedure the area looked like a gun-shot wound and, my God, it was painful. I was angry that this spider had got away with it. Usually they only bite when you lean on them or sit on them, which often leads to their demise. I was pissed off that this one was still at large; I thought briefly about finding it, but I'd never know for sure that it was the same one.

The doctors told me afterwards that had I not been treated when I was, I could have lost my leg. They also told me that I was stupid for not seeking treatment sooner. I would have, but I didn't know I had been bitten!

I have a bad scar on the outside of my ankle, but at least I have a cool story to go with it. Nowadays I actually have a relatively toned down fear of arachnids. In England the spiders are pathetic; they don't scare me any more.

# JOHN ROSE...

## ... ON SERVING A SENTENCE IN ONE OF THE WORLD'S MOST SAVAGE PRISONS

*'Seeing all this cruelty and not being able to speak to anyone sent me slowly mad. I was completely cut off from the outside world, only allowed to send and receive one letter a month. Even then the letters would all be censored and often came through with most of it scored out by guards. It was in one of these rare letters I was told that my mother had died. It was the worst moment of my life — stuck in Osaka Prison and discovering that the woman I had looked after for so long had died without me being there.'*

The second I opened my mouth I knew I'd ballsed up. The worst thing you could do in Osaka Prison was make noise. You would only speak when you were spoken to, and otherwise kept your mouth firmly shut. I didn't even know the name of the man in the next cell to me. But that day I was halfway through my daily eight-hour shift of stuffing envelopes and I'd run out. Without thinking, I called out to the guard. I'll never forget his face as he ran towards me. I'd already seen them kill at least one other prisoner and, the way he grabbed me, I assumed that I would be next. He dragged me by the neck across the prison's factory and past the other prisoners who kept silently working, staring at their envelopes and pretending they didn't know what was going on.

I was struggling to breathe by the time he got me over to the welding area. It all happened very fast. He grabbed a piece of red-hot metal, turned me round and pressed it into my back. The pain was indescribable. My skin literally sizzled as he held it there for what seemed like hours. When he'd finished branding me, he dragged me back to my table. Dazed, I sat down and started stuffing envelopes. I could feel my back melting.

In 2002 I was in a terrible state. I'd been in Thailand for five years and at first it was like paradise. Back in England, I'd spent twenty years working in terrible jobs while looking after my sick mother. I needed something different and Thailand was it. I got good work as an English teacher, made lots of friends and fell in love with a local girl.

In 2002 they changed the visa rules, which meant I couldn't get work. Within weeks I was skint. It was then that I met an Israeli guy in a bar. He explained that he was a drug dealer – but only marijuana, not heroin or anything like that. He told me that drugs were very expensive in Japan and offered me £4,000 to carry 4 kilos of marijuana there for him. I agreed pretty much immediately. I saw it as my only chance to get enough money to stay in Thailand and sort out my visa.

A few days later I was in Fukuoka Airport in Japan, picking up my suitcase from the carousel. The drugs were sewn into the lining. I was pretty calm, especially when I saw there weren't any sniffer dogs. What I didn't know was that they had a system where they pulled out maybe every tenth person from the security queue. Sure enough, they called me over and emptied everything out of my suitcase. I still thought I'd get away with it, but then the guard held up the empty suitcase. With horror, I could see what he was thinking – it was far too heavy. He just looked at me and smiled. I was fucked.

I learned pretty quickly what it was going to be like to be banged up in Japan. They stuck me in a detention centre and began what they called their 'investigation'. I confessed everything, but that didn't seem to matter. For six weeks they interviewed me for twelve hours a day. They started from the day I was born and just trawled through my life. If I said one thing differently then they would start shouting, slapping me and spitting at me.

I got my first proper 'going over' when a guard walked past my cell and saw that I was looking out of the window. I didn't realise that you had to look at the floor whenever a guard was in your presence. A few of them came into my cell and gave me a good kicking. I was in shock. I knew I'd been mad to carry drugs, but I just couldn't believe the brutality. What's more, I couldn't tell anyone about it. When someone from the British Consulate came to visit me, there were four English-speaking guards and two translators in the room with us. The message was pretty clear; don't say a word about anything.

I didn't go into the trial with much confidence but the judge was probably the only decent man I encountered during the whole process. He explained to me everything that was going on and he gave me four years. It could have been a lot worse. I actually felt relieved. I didn't realise at the time what four years in a Japanese prison would mean. I remember thinking that maybe they had been trying to scare me in the detention centre and prison would be better. When I walked into the prison, I realised that had been wishful thinking. There were hundreds of prisoners, but you could have heard a pin drop. It was incredible – total silence. That was the rule.

Every single guard was a sick, sadistic bastard. As a matter of course they spat in the faces of prisoners, slapped us and kept us up at night by banging on our doors every hour or so. There was one American guy in for drug charges who got beaten up almost every day. I was the same; they were quick to call me a 'filthy foreigner' and 'drugs scum'. I tried my best to avoid doing anything that might provoke them, but there were so many rules that it was impossible not to cross them sooner or later. For example, we were given one bar of soap a week. At the end of my first week, as they inspected my cell, I still had some soap left. Big mistake; I should have binned the tiny scrap. The guards started screaming, pressed the alarm button and dragged me to the floor. They put me into handcuffs and leg irons and made me eat the soap in front of them. Then they took me to the 'investigation cell'. This was the one place in the prison that everyone dreaded. It was one metre square, with no windows and a light on twenty-four hours a day. You could just about sit down and were only allowed out for half an hour a day.

The guards used the investigation cell for their mind games. They threw one person in there randomly every day and they never told you how long you would be there. During the first time I was there, I asked the guard how long I'd got. He told me six months. That just ruins your mind. In fact I got out after three days, but they were by far the longest three days of my life.

By day we worked in the prison factory. First we were marched in naked and they would pull some of us over for deliberately painful cavity searches. We would get into our uniforms and be lined up to chant our apologies. 'I apologise for my unforgivable criminality. It is due to my criminality that I am here.'

Then we'd start stuffing envelopes. It was the most mind-numbing job you can imagine. We had to keep our noses six to eight inches above the desks and not look anywhere except for the envelopes. That was for eight hours a day, sometimes longer. It sent you mad. I daydreamed to get through it and I must have been miles away the day I called out to the guard for more envelopes. I didn't make that mistake again.

I was lucky to just be branded and scarred for life. One prisoner snapped in the factory, grabbed a guard and banged his head on a pillar. There was this horrible pause before fifty guards went for him. They put him in a straitjacket and left him in the investigation cell, badly beaten. Every day for twenty-three days, they let him out for an hour to clean up and exercise then they would put him back in. On the twenty-third day he died.

Seeing all this cruelty and not being able to speak to anyone sent me slowly mad. I was completely cut off from the outside world, only allowed to send and receive one letter a month. Even then the letters would all be censored and often came through with most of it scored out by the guards. It was in one of these rare letters I was told that my mother had died. It was the worst moment of my life – stuck in Osaka Prison and discovering that the woman I had looked after for so long had died without me being there.

After Osaka Prison you would think that I would be on the straight and narrow for the rest of my life. But unfortunately that is not the case. Nine months after being released, after trying and failing to get honest work in England, I found myself standing in Lille train station in France with a bag full of ecstasy tablets. The sniffer dog came round the corner and that was me caught again. I did nearly a year in a French prison, and compared to Japan it was a holiday camp. I'd go as far as to say I enjoyed it. There was lots of sunbathing, reading and time to reflect. I got out and this time I can say with confidence that I've changed. I'm back in Thailand now and living an honest life.

Recently I ran into an old face who offered me £10,000 for a day's drugs work. I turned it down. I've done my last job for these people. I was never any bloody good at it.

# BEVERLI RHODES...

## ... ON HER ESCAPE FROM THE 7 JULY LONDON BOMBINGS

*'I was shocked by what I saw that morning. It really was like Barbie dolls getting broken and crushed — just bits of people. I always perceived humans to be more resilient but, in actual fact, we are very fragile.'*

On that morning we were rushing like hell; we had to actually swerve and cut in front of a bus so that I could jump out at the station and dash through to get my train. The company I worked for was just off Tavistock Square, that's where I was heading.

It was murky, damp and unseasonably cool for the time of year. It was Thursday 7 July 2005. A day that was set to host the deadliest bombings in London since the Luftwaffe hit the city.

That morning, day two of the G8 Summit and just a day after London won the 2012 Olympic bid, the Metropolitan Police responded to incidents at six locations on the Underground and one on a bus. There were three blasts on the Underground meaning that survivors emerged from stations either end of each incident, hence the initial reports of six explosions on trains. This was Al Qaeda's debut in London and their standard was high; it was dirty and ugly.

I have very iffy bits of memory from the day. The last real thing I remember clearly was rushing to get the train. I can vaguely recall putting my laptop between my feet on the floor, the very same company computer that contained the presentation I was on my way to give for the 2012 Olympics' hard- and soft-ring security. I had my handbag out and I put on some lipstick. I was getting ready to get off. I usually give my seat up a couple of stops early so I can get myself to the door. I had been travelling into town so much for work so I had just fallen into a routine; get up, head for the door and get ready to get off but, of course, none of that happened.

When I came round I was trying to focus; desperately trying to work out what on earth had happened. I was groggy and confused. I could feel my heart beating. I could hear my blood pumping. Terrified, I tried to gather my surroundings. I have been told that I was unconscious for around ten to twelve minutes. I started to remember that I was on a train, on my way to work. Apart from the distant ringing in my ears, I heard nothing; a deathly silence. Then I heard a low, soft and terrible screaming coming from somewhere in the tunnel. I heard my voice and others saying, 'Don't panic, keep calm.' Disorientated, unable to see or breathe, as if I had been plunged into the very bowels of the earth, I struggled to my feet.

When the bomb went off, the train shuddered to a dead stop and I was flung forward. I smashed face first into the long pole next to the door. I felt a tremendous heat in my head and on the left hand side of my body. I noticed that I was very sticky on the left hand side of my face. There was a strange feeling in my mouth, which I can only describe as like chewing a sponge. I felt feverishly with my tongue. There was a searing, burning pain in my jaw. My mouth was full of teeth. I didn't know that, ideally, in that situation you should spit your teeth out. With what little strength I had left, I foolishly squashed all my broken teeth back into place. I now know that this was actually the worst thing I could have done because I had inadvertently introduced foreign bodies and a really awful infection into my gums and jaw.

There were a lot of women around and we realised that what was coming into the train was smoke. There was no visibility. When I looked down I could only see as far as my knees. We all decided to hold hands and start praying, just in case we were not saved. I remember actively thinking about speaking to my family – had I told my girls and my partner that I loved them? It was like doing a mental stocktake of the emotional wreckage in my life. I was making sure that, if I was going to, I was ready to die. Because I was unconscious for so long it is hard to say how long we were in that train, but I would guess around thirty to forty minutes. It felt a lot longer.

I am a security consultant for the protection of critical and national infrastructure; anything crucial like roads, railways, bridges, the Underground, container cargo ships, docks, hospitals, schools etc. My area of expertise is assuring resilience and securing the buildings and installations that are essential to keep the country running. I used to put together protection measures for utilities, gas, water, electricity and basically anything that could be hit by a terrorist group, an arsonist or even just a person with an axe to grind to cause tremendous disruption. As a result of my background and training I soon realised that it didn't have any signatures of a fire, which was the buzz on the train. People were being told that it was just a fire caused by an electrical fault. We were told not to worry; that there was an electrical surge at King's Cross that had caused a fire. I knew it was definitely a bomb. I was also worried that the smoke within the deep tunnels, which are up to 30 m below the surface, would have nowhere to go. The tunnels are 3.5 m in diameter with about 15 cm clearance around the train – a claustrophobic environment at the best of times.

Using the light from our mobile phones, we just managed to make each other out. Although incredibly nauseous from the amount of blood I had swallowed, I composed myself. Those of us who could still walk moved forward in single file as the driver forced open his door and helped us off the train. Black with soot and dazed in shock, we staggered down the smoky tunnel. We were helping one another, encouraging each other to keep going – we were nearly out. I was shocked by what I saw that morning. It really was like Barbie dolls getting broken and crushed – just bits of people. I always perceived humans to be more resilient but, in actual fact, we are very fragile.

The bravery and kindness of the ambulance and hospital staff is not in doubt. But when twenty survivors and I struggled out of that tunnel at 9.20 a.m. we were not met by the medical attention that was promised. We found scenes of confusion; shocked London Underground staff and bemused commuters as far as the eye could see. We were told to contact the police to register once we had received medical attention. I had thought that London was a resilient and well-prepared city but neither its intelligence service nor its civil protection can provide 100 per cent security.

I think we had all become a bit feverish in our bid to get out as quickly as possible and it was an immense relief to get to the surface. We expected a lot more than we found, though. We expected loud hailers and overhead messages from the station. There was none of that. It was just chaotic.

Word got around that there had been other bombs in the city. We realised quickly that there would be many deaths and we considered ourselves the lucky ones. I was with two other ladies from the train. We didn't think we were wounded sufficiently to warrant taking up the precious time of medics and hospitals. Especially my injuries, it was just facial and teeth. At the time I believed my private medical insurance with AXA would cover it; I wrongly assumed that I could claim for my injuries. So we pooled our money together and decided we would look for a taxi and let the emergency services deal with the people who were critically injured.

We found a black cab. The driver said that because of what was happening he only wanted cash; he wanted to get out of London as quickly as possible. We managed to scrape together about £46 between us. With that money he was able to take us to the top of the A10 in North London. I was hoping to go and get medical attention but Chase Farm Hospital would have been a lot more than £46 in the taxi. The moment the metre reached £46 that was it; he stopped the cab and said, 'Out ya get.'

I was shocked. We looked like shit; we were covered in soot and dust and by that time my face had swollen, so I looked like a hamster. He wasn't having any of it, he said he was leaving us there and going home. That's where he dropped us off; right there on the side of the road, like a black bag of dirty washing.

Not a single person on the A10 stopped. No cars pulled over to work out why these three, obviously injured, ladies were stumbling down the side of the road. It was like people were just looking past us. It was still before midday so a lot of people driving along may not have known what had actually occurred in town. At that time even the news wasn't clear about exactly what had happened – nothing had been confirmed. Most of those motorists didn't know that these three women, who looked like they had been dragged through a hedge backwards, were actually survivors from the train bombings.

It became almost impossible to make mobile phone calls. The mobile networks did not work in the first hours after the bombings. I noticed hundreds of frantic people desperately trying to get a connection, anxious to find out what had happened to loved ones. Since that day I have heard dozens of painful accounts from fellow survivors of how they were unable to contact their families and friends.

Sceptics believe that the networks were deliberately closed down. If so, was that for fear of terrorists using mobile phones to detonate bombs? We would like to know so we can understand and forgive some of the lonely agonies of that morning.

One of the ladies I was with on the A10, a nineteen-year-old, was getting increasingly distraught and upset. She had started her first working week on the Monday. She was worried she was going to get fired for not turning up. She was cold from shock so I gave her my jumper and told her that she probably wouldn't lose her job as being blown up on a train would be deemed a reasonable excuse to miss work.

The young girl finally managed to get through to her mum on her mobile, which was amazing, so her mum came and got her. We all parted ways. I turned off and started heading towards my house in Enfield in the hope that I would be able to get there on foot.

My partner was at work when her admin staff in the Audiology department at the hospital informed her about what had happened. She had dropped me off at the station so she knew I was on one of these trains. She left everything and came looking for me. She literally ran out of work the moment she realised what was happening.

She drove around frantically searching for me. She eventually found me walking along the side of the road; I wasn't on the pavement any more, I was following the lines. I was still very dazed. Rather than taking the short cuts, I was following the same roads that I would have been on had I been driving. That's how she found me.

Firstly we went home, where I cleaned myself up a bit. I looked in the mirror at the state of my mouth to evaluate the damage. Already the smell had started; the infection and swelling was getting worse as time passed. We phoned the NHS for advice on my injuries. They were obviously inundated with calls and following their advice we headed to the hospital.

A & E was absolute chaos. I remember sitting there watching the survivors pour in as the panicked staff struggled with the injuries. It was literally like a stampede, but of people – victims of the attacks.

All my operations have been done privately at the Phyathai Hospital in Bangkok, Thailand. I couldn't wait endless months for the procedure to be done through the NHS. My dentist told me that I wasn't really going to be able to wait around and advised me to get the infection cleared as soon as possible. I managed to have the first round of treatment for the infections sorted in August. Luckily, the Red Cross paid for me to have the surgery done for which I am very grateful. My surgeon booked a two-hour slot in the operating theatre, but because there was so much debris in there and the infection was so severe it actually took closer to five hours.

There were about eight or nine teeth that were shattered, cracked or split. The jaw itself had become like Swiss cheese; full of lots of little holes due to the severity of the infection because I was silly enough to squash my teeth back in along with all the stuff that was floating around in the carriage. The pain from the infection was unbelievable – the worst pain I have ever felt in my life; I would rather give birth.

Now I have implants. I bit an apple recently and had to check that I actually had. It is a very strange sensation; there is no feeling in them. My Christmas dinner in 2005 was a piece of soft bloomer bread with squashed up roast potato, finely cut turkey and bits of vegetables smothered in gravy, which took me forty-five minutes to eat.

My life is completely and utterly different to what it used to be. I look different now to how I looked before 7 July. I used to have almost black hair but because of the shock it has lost its colour. I would say about sixty per cent of my hair is white and the rest still has some dark brown in it. I didn't know that when there is a shock-induced loss of pigmentation it stays that way; you don't go back to your own colour. Within the first year my hair turned white and handfuls of it started to come out. Part of the hair died from the impact or the shock, I am not sure which.

When I was going through the Home Office in January 2006 and they were deciding what they could do for the survivors and how they were going to help, I decided that more needed to be done for us. There are so many of us, not only survivors but also the families of those that survived and of those who didn't. It is necessary to have some form of compassion and understanding, and some kind of organisation that can offer assistance mentally, physically and emotionally. A lot of people suffer badly from survivor's guilt; a lot feel they should have died. Unfortunately, a lot of survivors have killed themselves in the last four years because of this guilt. Part of the Survivor's Coalition Foundation, which I am a part of, is to have a list of all of us and then we have a round robin where we phone each other to make sure we are all OK. If there are any people we are particularly worried about, we will phone them, or on occasions go and meet them, just to talk things through. This can be immensely helpful.

I have been on trains over land since the incident but I cannot get onto the Underground. I haven't been on one since that day. My goal by the fifth anniversary is to be able to go down and stand on a platform, which is going to be some feat; just to stand there without going into an episode is going to be quite hard for me. I can manage to walk past the entrances now but the moment I smell that familiar Underground smell it is like an assault on my senses and I just can't handle it. I have to get myself to the stage where I can walk in, ignore the smells, go through the turnstiles and see how I feel walking down the stairs. I am not sure if I will be able to manage it but I am going to try and see how I do. I take my hat off to the survivors who have managed to go on the Underground since but I just can't do it yet.

On the second anniversary people were putting flowers down in Russell Square Station and my partner and I attended. I was standing on the other side of the road directly opposite the station's entrance and I just went ballistic; there was absolutely no way on God's green earth that I was going to be able to walk across and put flowers down. We ended up going to the main park where the anniversary ceremony was happening to pay our respects. I just couldn't go back to that station.

Many of the people I have spoken to are full of practical suggestions to improve the response to the aftermath of a disaster, stressing to me that their want for a public inquiry is out of a desire to get something positive from the events. We've talked about the communication between carriages, or lack of it, and whether each carriage or the train driver should carry first aid kits, torches and hammers to smash windows. Whether breathing apparatus should be kept in stations for rescue workers and whether there should be guards on trains.

In the days and weeks that followed, many survivors were left alone, traumatised and isolated. A Family Assistance Centre was set up in Victoria after the bombings. Survivors who dropped in talked positively of this resource. But the name misled many who thought it was only for families of the dead and so never availed themselves of its facilities, which included counsellors, victim support staff and representatives from the Red Cross, Salvation Army, social workers and volunteers.

Later the centre, renamed as the '7th July Assistance Centre', moved to smaller premises. But the Data Protection Act meant that all survivors and families who had registered under the old name had to be deleted from the database. Many survivors were left in the dark once more.

It was us, the workers and the general public, that were targets, not politicians or those in power. We are just ordinary people, the people that keep the country going – maintaining financial stability, the workers of our land. On 7 July we were treated like soldiers in a war. Why were we targeted?

I have been impressed over the months at the commitment of survivors to try and make things better; helping each other back on the Tube; acting as 'travel buddies'; emailing supportive messages and other positive actions taken to help each other.

But there is also anger at the perceived lack of help, suspicion about what the government may be trying to hide and frustration that, despite repeated claims from politicians that they speak 'for the victims', victims' voices are not being heard.

I wonder sometimes how we as human beings can endure the rise in intensity within our lives when faced with such a traumatic event, but somehow we do. Recovery from the bombings is emotionally challenging for all of us and now I feel like I am being forced to serve a sentence, without committing a crime. My sentence is to live with this for the rest of my life.

We were just going about our daily jobs and now our lives will never be the same again. For generations people will recall the events of that day and look at the lack of joined-up thinking of radical terrorists.

My life is not yet normal. I still have the nightmares and am still struggling to recover entirely. Things have moved forward in an unusual way, I am now taking master classes called 'Hate, Hope & Healing', which allows all participants to deal with their inner hate, consider their aspirations and then finally help them move forward with their lives.

I hope that some day I will fully recover from the horrors of 7 July 2005.

*'All that is necessary for evil to succeed is that good men do nothing.'* – Edmund Burke

# SINCLAIR BEECHAM...

## ... ON HIS RAGS-TO-RICHES STORY OF FOUNDING PRET A MANGER

*'Then a great friend of mine from college rang me up and offered me the opportunity to go into business with him. This was a chance I was grateful for and one that I grabbed with both hands... So that was it: in 1986, at the age of twenty-eight, I left my job and we started Pret A Manger.'*

I left school with virtually no qualifications besides some very bad A levels. I passed English and Economics, just, and managed to fail French twice; I think the second failure was actually worse than the first. I didn't go to university and I ended up working as a cashier at a high street bank, which I absolutely hated. After some time I decided that I really needed to get a different job; I knew that much. I went to Marks and Spencer for an interview with their Management Training Scheme and I turned up with a very bad hangover. Understandably, and rather appropriately, they didn't employ me – even if I hadn't had the hangover I suspect they still wouldn't have.

The next plan was a similar role, this time in the Littlewoods Management Training Scheme. After attending one of their assessment days, I was offered the job and went to their busiest shop on Oxford Street. I quickly realised that it wasn't for me. That was a life-changing moment.

When I realised that I wasn't where I wanted to be, I knew I had to do something else. Knowing that I had to do something else was one thing but now I had to decide what that 'something else' was going to be.

I had been successful in getting the job with Littlewoods but didn't want to accept the role. So I had to up my game otherwise I wasn't going to get anywhere near where I wanted to be. After lots of thought I went to university where I took a vocational degree. I am not at all academically minded and the idea of taking an academic course was a truly depressing prospect. I ended up taking a degree in Urban Estate Management at the Polytechnic of Central London, latterly called – rather grandly – the University of Westminster. After university I ended up working with a property developer, Crest Nicholson, which was a really good job with great prospects and was a position that I really enjoyed.

Then a great friend of mine from college rang me up and offered me the opportunity to go into business with him. This was a chance I was grateful for and one that I grabbed with both hands. I had had other new business offers around that time, which I had not taken up. Julian was my best mate at college, so it seemed to me that it was the right option.

So that was it: in 1986, at the age of twenty-eight, I left my job and we started Pret A Manger. The first shop, on Victoria Street, is still there today. The second shop, in Holborn, wasn't opened until four years later.

I would say we were pretty much destitute for that four-year period. Julian and I worked in that first shop every day; we were serving customers every lunchtime. I was making deliveries, pushing a trolley around an office building and we were working as hard as we could to make it successful.

We were both tired; it was a really tough time for us. All of our friends, who were working as investment bankers and things like that, were earning enormous amounts of money and I couldn't even afford to put petrol in the office van; my only vehicle. I started to wonder what on earth I was doing. I had a very good friend whose house I was living in at the time, and for eighteen months he didn't once ask me for the rent.

I suspect there would have come a time when we might have given up; perhaps if we had actually become bankrupt, which we were perilously close to doing for quite a long time. Otherwise, we were determined to win. I guess in life you've got to be determined to beat the odds.

We didn't have a traditional business plan; this is probably why it took us so long to get the first shop right. Julian and I weren't caterers but rather we were customers. We both knew instinctively what was right for our customer. We didn't know how to make money and we didn't know how to run a business, but we knew what a discerning customer wanted, so we made sure we provided exactly that. Our whole business concept was to provide what the customer wanted, then work out how to make money out of it. Eventually, we did!

Despite everything during that period, we stuck at it. I was lucky to be partnered with Julian as we had complementary skills; if I was good at something he was almost certainly bad and vice versa. In the early days we did everything together;

it was great fun. The trouble was that, at the beginning, the two of us were less value than one person.

When we learned we had different skills, we played to our strengths and Pret really started to take off; we both added value to the company at different times. We were lucky in many ways but we were especially fortunate to have each other. Together we slowly but surely developed a great business and worked at it harder and for longer than anyone could imagine. We teetered on the knife-edge of bankruptcy but, despite the odds, we persevered. Towards the end of that four-year period our business started to come good and it finally all started to make sense. I could even pay myself almost enough to live on. Up until that moment neither of us had taken anything out of the business.

We began planning a second shop, but nobody would lend us any money until, eventually, we found a private equity lender who said he would give us ninety per cent of the money. This meant he would be leaving us pretty tight and he also wanted fifty per cent of the equity. It struck me that I was going to have to work twice as hard as I had been to achieve the same return. There seemed little point in doing that, so we said, 'Thanks, but no thanks.'

We struggled on, trying to secure an investor for the second shop. Eventually we got lucky with a man from the Midland Bank, now HSBC, who lent us the money and perhaps shouldn't have because at that point we were not a truly bankable proposition. Luckily for us, this man thought we were – thank heavens! We will always remember him fondly.

We finally opened the second shop and it became an instant success. There have been a number of very lucky breaks in Pret's history but meeting this man at the Midland Bank was certainly one of the luckiest. We repaid that money in full in somewhere between fifteen and eighteen months and we have been a good customer to that bank ever since. In fact, the Business Banking Manager we deal with today was that man's assistant.

This funding enabled us to open the second shop, third, fourth and fifth, which all happened relatively quickly. The second shop was opened in April 1990 and the fifth shop was up and running by May 1991. We had always planned to open more stores, as I don't think one shop would have ever satisfied us. If we had been unable to open another shop, I honestly don't know what either of us would have done.

When it came to the sixth shop, the bank said no. Our man had left and his replacement refused to lend us the money. So I summoned him in rather an arrogant and perhaps aggressive way to one of our shops in London. He turned up and within twenty minutes he was a believer. We have had support from HSBC ever since. You really do need the support of a good bank when you are growing a business. A bank is as good as their relationships and the fact that we are still banking with them to this day is a credit to us both.

Pret has evolved. It has been polished and refined a lot over the years. The first shop took a lot of work but by the time the second shop opened we were doing virtually what Pret does today. There are 200 stores in the UK and around thirty in New York and Hong Kong. I am a non-executive director with a seat on the board, and I am the biggest private shareholder. In 2008 we sold a majority stake in the business to a private equity firm, Bridgeport Capital.

Somebody once said that head-hunters have all sorts of categories that they put people into when considering them for employment. I have been told there is a 'category thirteen', which is basically unemployable for all sorts of reasons. I think many entrepreneurs are in that category and I suspect people wouldn't doubt that I am category thirteen – I am unemployable.

My drive was never about the financial rewards. I think it always had something to do with wanting to be independent and wanting to win. It is difficult to remember over twenty years ago what really first lit my fire but I know I always had an instinct to run my own business.

In later life I would say that money was the score not the motivator; success is the motivator. When you start as a twenty-eight-year-old in a business, on your own, there is no money; in fact there is less than no money. Don't get me wrong, money is nice but it's not the goal, it was not the purpose. We didn't set out to make cash; we set out to create a business. If I was entirely motivated by money, I probably wouldn't have left the security of a good job with great prospects at Crest.

Even when we were profitable, we ploughed everything back into the business and invested in its growth. That's why we paid off that first debt in fifteen months. Most people would have taken the five-year term and paid it off normally but we were determined to clear the debt. When we took our first money out in 2001 we must have had about seventy-five shops and we had never taken any money out of the business previously.

We have always worked sensibly with our cash; perhaps this explains why it has been so successful. I think if it were all about money we would have done what lots of people do when they make their first buck. We would have gone out and bought a Ferrari, blown the cash and maybe ended up bankrupt, like a lot of those people who buy their first Ferrari a little too early. We were the antithesis of that.

Nowadays, I am spending most of my time working on hotels. I recently opened The Hoxton in London. I was hoping to open others but then we had the massive economic crash, or 'credit crunch' as they call it. So I pulled out of every deal I was doing.

I have always hated hotels; I think they are often such bad value for their customers. They seem to rip their guests off and get away with it. Staying in a hotel is just like sitting in a taxi in a traffic jam; watching the meter tick over but not going anywhere. There is another way and that is what we are trying to do with The Hoxton.

When I am staying in a hotel I can't bring myself to open the $8 bottle of water because it is such a rip-off and it goes so against the grain. I often remove the contents of the minibar and then go down to the local shop and buy a bottle of water and a six-pack of beer as it's much cheaper. What sort of business makes its customers behave like that and doesn't think there is something wrong with it?

I was recently in New York and they charged me a dollar a minute to make a local phone call. Local phone calls in New York are free.

I hate the revenue management system in hotels. They are like airlines, charging everyone a different price and scheming to work out how to take your last dime. It has no integrity.

We have a filter that we put everything through. If it would piss me off as a customer or if it is a rip-off, we will not do it. It's a straightforward judgment. Is an $8 bottle of water a rip-off? Yes. Does it piss you off when they get your bills wrong? Yes. Does it piss you off when they try and charge you $7 for a beer? Yes. Is it a rip-off when you pay a quid a minute to phone America? Yes.

It is a simple system but it seems to work. The hotel is running at about ninety-five per cent occupancy. It is even full on a Sunday night and people write lots of nice things about it, so I guess we must be doing something right.

Business is all about people. Right now, for example, there are 3,000 plus staff in Pret stores taking care of customers. My role is to motivate people to do a better job. If it is fun, like we've tried to make it at Pret, people do a better job than they otherwise would. If everyone is having fun, then we all win. I think this is applicable to all types of business. In fact, one of the things we put in our budget is 'FUN'. If we don't spend the fun budget, I am not happy. There are lots of things we do to make sure everyone involved is having fun.

Hindsight is a great thing; there are a lot of things we could have done better in those early days and there are a lot of things we didn't know about that we learned the hard way. As you get older, your appetite for risk changes. The more of your net worth you have in one business the less desire you have to risk it. Therefore it was important for our business that we did sell a significant share of it when we did. It is important that the next generation can be allowed to get hold of it to take it to the next level. I think towards the end we were holding it back because there were opportunities that perhaps we missed.

I now want to make decisions that are not risky, as opposed to at the beginning where we took some massively risky decisions that luckily came good. We wouldn't do things like that today. I think when you want to move a business on you need to change the structure, to give it a new lease of life. Giving the younger people involved new opportunities with new positions is vital and I think that is working very well with Pret today.

I must have been a bit of a dreamer; you wouldn't set out on your own if you weren't, although we never would have imagined in our wildest dreams that the business would become as successful as it has.

When does it need to change again? I don't know. What will it look like when it does? I don't know. All I know for sure is that I will stay on board as long as it is fun and as long as I can add value.

# MICHELLE BOWATER...

## ... ON LOSING FIFTEEN STONE TO HAVE A BABY AGAINST ALL ODDS

*'Becoming a mother is the most phenomenal experience and something that has always been out of my reach until now. I am also the first woman in Britain to have a baby after a gastric bypass and the fitting of a gastric band. We made history.'*

I am not a smoker, drug taker, alcoholic or serial killer. The only thing I am guilty of is being a 'cereal' slimmer and, wow, what a journey the last thirty-seven years have been.

I was born 29 March 1972, around Easter time. I was a 6 lb 7 oz healthy baby with big blue eyes and dimples. I was the first child to an ordinary Midlands couple. My twin brothers were born in 1974 and my sister in 1976. My mother had four children all under the age of four to look after and no doubt it was a nightmare for her.

One of my earliest memories is sitting in my highchair, where I remember crying uncontrollably and being given a huge chunk of white bread – the size of my head – covered in lashings of 'best' butter. I was only eight months old but I enjoyed every last bit of that bread, to the point where every time I cried I was given the 'treat' again. So the habit started... I cried, got the bread, I cried, got the bread. I remember I used to start crying because I knew I would be given bread and butter, not because there was anything wrong with me. That is where my food addiction began.

My childhood was a miserable one. I was constantly 'fed' by my parents, grandparents, lollipop lady and anyone else who thought this little round ball was cute. Everyone around me – the bastards feeding me up – talked all the time about my 'puppy fat'. I was told it would all disappear by the time I was thirteen – yeah right!

We were a poor family. My mum had six mouths to feed and, from an early age, I realised she too had issues with food. She was always on some form of diet – the most memorable being the 'cereal diet'. For six months all she ate was cereal and didn't lose a pound; she just spent a lot of time on the loo. I was put on the same diet for two months when I was twelve. I failed miserably as I was eating about eight bowls of cheap cereal every day. I even turned to stealing food from my classmates' lunch boxes because mine always contained a plastic bowl, spoon and two Weetabix; not the most appealing lunch. It didn't help that the bowl had Bungle from the TV show *Rainbow* all over it. It was the only one we had and so – you've guessed it – I was called Bungle for the last year in middle school.

Every day I cried on my walk home, both from the pain in my legs, due to the two-mile walk, and because of the abuse I was receiving at school. I always hated physical activity and I can't stand cereal now, even twenty-five years on!

At the age of thirteen I didn't lose my puppy fat like I had been told I would. I started secondary school, my parents divorced – forcing me to become a substitute mother for my siblings – and I began turning more and more to food for comfort.

Secondary school was hard work as I was gaining a stone in weight for every year I was there. At thirteen stone I was the 'biggest' kid in school. I wasn't called 'Bungle' any more, though; oh no, some spotty, ugly schoolboy thought it would be hilarious to call me 'Titanic' instead. A name that stuck to me like glue for three years!

My parents' divorce did come as a shock to me. They always seemed so happy but in actual fact my father had been having affairs whilst working from home. Eventually my mother decided to get rid of him and since then I have only seen him three times. At this time in my life I was suddenly thrown into 'motherhood' as my mum had to work four jobs to survive and provide us kids with food and clothes etc. So, being the eldest, I took over the household chores. I was doing all the cleaning, cooking and caring for my siblings, and I hated every minute of it. I was angry as my childhood was being taken away. Whilst my siblings were all out with friends during the six-week summer holidays, I was stuck at home playing 'house'. At this point I started to eat more and more out of boredom and frustration as well as comfort. Food became my crutch, my best friend and something I relied on in good times and bad. No one else would listen to me but the Wagon Wheels were always there in my hour of need!

I was a mature-looking thirteen-year-old; I looked more like sixteen. A friend of mine arranged a blind date for me with a boy she knew. I thought, 'Why not?' I had never really thought about boys until then as I was indoors most of the time. He was eighteen, so a lot older than me. I told him my name was Lois (like off *Superman*) as it enabled me to leave my world for a short while and enter a fantasy. But I wish I hadn't.

I had been seeing him for around two weeks before he tried anything sexual with me and because I was so young and naive I didn't really know what he was doing until it was too late. I said no, but he carried on. His brother finally saved me after hearing my screams. I became aware that I had to protect myself from anything like this ever happening again. I went home, never said a word to anyone about it and got on with my life. Even now, recalling this memory brings me to tears. I had locked this part of my life away in a box and had forgotten about it – it's only now that I realise the demons will always be with me.

What I did in the next three years was eat and eat and eat. I had to make myself as unattractive as possible to ensure nothing like this happened to me ever again and, thankfully, it worked! I threw myself into funding my addiction; working three jobs as well as looking after the house. I had two babysitting jobs and a newspaper round. I spent all the money I earned on sweets, chocolates, crisps and anything else I wanted.

My mother soon realised that I had a problem with food when she found all my wrappers under my mattress. So she dragged me along to my first slimming club. It was full of lots of very sad, miserable women 'battling the bulge'. I tried to stick to the diet; at least it wasn't a faddy one like the cereal diet that I had done the year before. Despite having no willpower I tried my hardest and in the first three weeks I managed to lose 14 lb. Then family members started saying how great it was to see me looking so beautiful again. In response to the positive feedback I started to eat once again to prevent getting unwanted attention, which was one of the reasons for my weight gain in the first place.

So for the next three years I ate myself into a miserable world. By the time I left school I weighed seventeen stone and was still being called 'Titanic' by the not-so-spotty schoolboy et al. I left school with five GCSEs and was lucky enough to get a job in the Inland Revenue as a Revenue Assistant. I was the youngest employee in the tax office for three years and was mothered by all the other women with whom I worked. My day was filled with P45s, gossip and cream cakes; I loved every minute of it!

Earning my own money meant I could give some to my mum to help her with the bills. My siblings had gone to live with their dad at this point so it was just my mum and me. She was out most nights and I stayed in, ordering takeaway food and eating myself into oblivion. I became an even bigger secret eater; I used to buy food at the supermarket on the way home and hide it in my handbag. I would eat my dinner at night and then when mum went out I would attack the food I had bought that afternoon. When I was finished I would hide the wrappers; I was ashamed of the hold food had over me. If mum didn't go out for any reason, I used to get so angry. She never knew it was because I couldn't eat the food; she must have just thought I was a moody cow!

One night whilst mum was out, my friend Rita and I shared a bottle of wine, got a bit tipsy and placed a lonely-hearts ad in the local newspaper. I didn't want to beat around the bush when I described myself so I said I was 'cuddly'. What it should have said was 'humongous' (If I could have spelled it, I would have written it). At that time I weighed twenty-one stone and I was miserable. I had a great job and I worked with lots of lovely people, but I was fat.

Anyway, after a week I checked to see if I had any messages from any potential dates and, to my surprise, I did have one. I met him in 1995 and five years later, when I was twenty-eight years old, we got married. I guess the main reason I married this man is because he had the same food addiction as me, and we got fat together. It was a comfortable life and I felt safe for the first time, but the sex was terrible. I still had hang-ups about what had happened to me at thirteen. I never addressed the issues; I had put that event into a box and locked it deep away inside.

We weighed forty-eight stone between us; I was twenty-five and he was twenty-three stone. He was 6 ft 7 in and I was 5 ft 3 in. We must have looked like a freak show.

I kept getting the same from people; everyone kept telling me I had a pretty face. When you are fat and your family and friends keep telling you that you have a pretty face, what they really mean is, 'You've got a pretty face – it's a shame about the rest of you.'

He was a great husband and put up with a lot from me. I struggled every day with my demons and the 'fat suit' didn't do me any favours. Weighing twenty-five stone I couldn't walk, I couldn't breathe, I was always hot and red in the face, my legs chaffed when I walked, my boobs rubbed together and I got sores. I guess the worst thing was I couldn't wash and dry myself in my nether regions. Therefore I had smelly bits that grew bacteria and, to top it all off, I was incontinent and had to wear a sanitary towel every day – the joys! I was thirty-two years old but I felt like I was only existing, not living.

We did try for a baby at one point but it was too difficult to have sex and, with PCOS (polycystic ovarian syndrome) brought on by being so overweight, I was told I would never have a baby. So I put it to the back of my mind and put all my efforts into building a career for myself. I drove nice cars, bought very expensive things – handbags and shoes etc.

– to fill the 'void' in my life. I had come from a very poor background and finally I was earning a great salary having worked myself through the grades in Human Resources at the Inland Revenue.

My life changed in June 2004. I was persuaded to go on holiday with two other couples who were in their forties. I hadn't been on holiday for years because the trauma of not fitting into an aeroplane seat and dealing with the heat abroad wasn't fun. We were going to a villa in Spain and I stupidly thought that's where we would stay all week.

The holiday started with a beautiful air hostess noting, as I walked sideways on to the plane, that I needed an extender belt, as the normal belt wouldn't go around my huge frame. She shouted down the aisle to another hostess to get the lady with the black cardigan (me) an extender belt. I wanted to hit her. But, sadly, she was right. I can't tell you how hard I tried to fit in that seat without the bloody bright orange thing wrapped around me. I tried so hard that I bruised my thighs. The first thing I did when I was strapped in was pull the food tray down to try to hide myself but, unfortunately, it didn't budge past my boobs. I then decided I felt air sick to avoid having the food and further embarrassment of having to tackle the facilities – there was no way I was going to go to the toilet!

The first night on holiday was when I decided once and for all that I had had enough of living in my body. I got stuck in a restaurant chair on a public walkway and the waiter and my husband had to yank me out of it, much to the amusement of everyone walking past. One little Spaniard even took some video footage. I am sure I was on a Spanish version of *You've Been Framed* that summer.

I had a panic attack that evening for the first time in my life. I was desperate to go home but everyone encouraged me to stay for the rest of the week. I sat in that villa praying for the week to be over. I started to think about how weight was affecting my life. I hadn't realised until then that I always referred to it in the third person; I used to make comments like, 'When *the* weight comes off...'

It was disabling my life and stopping me from doing so much. I was almost agoraphobic and I never socialised. I had even managed to cap my own career development as a HR Manager as I wouldn't go on any training courses because I couldn't travel on public transport. I seriously wondered what I was doing with my life. I had to do something, and fast.

On my return to the UK the first thing I looked at was booking myself into a fat camp. I also started searching the Internet for the 'magic pill'. I had tried absolutely everything over the last nineteen years; I had done all the diets, sensible and faddy ones (even attempting the dreaded cereal diet two more times). I had been to every single slimming club at least three times in the hope of conquering my weight battle, but at twenty-five stone it seemed too long a journey to start.

I then saw an advert for gastric banding, which is surgery for weight loss. I had never had an operation in my life and after I read up on this I thought, 'Well, I've done everything else'. It was the only thing left to try. I called the private clinic and three weeks later, at a 60.12 BMI and £8,000 lighter, I walked down to theatre in a gown, which was too small for me; showing everyone my bum crack. I left my dignity at the hospital door.

I was one of the first people in the UK to have a gastric band with this clinic. The operation was uncomfortable but not painful and I recovered well. I returned to work five days later and stuck to my post-operation regime of just liquids, and I started to see the weight come off.

Three months later I had lost three stone and I went for a review appointment at the clinic. They were really pleased with my progress and offered me a job talking about my experience to other patients. My confidence had grown, my self-esteem improved and I was up for the challenge. So on 14 February 2005 my life changed. I joined the company that had helped me so much and I was re-born.

Before I left my old company, though, I made sure I did one last thing. That spotty schoolboy who had called me 'Titanic' for all those years had coincidently ended up working at my company six months before I left. He wasn't spotty any more but was still just as ugly! He was constantly late for work so before I left I sacked him. Walking him off the premises was the best feeling ever!

Over a period of two years I lost ten stone in total, life was better, I could move more easily and I had gone from wearing size thirty-two clothes to size twenty. Surely this was enough for me?

However, I was still incontinent and was bigger than most patients coming for a surgical consultation. Work was getting tough as it had turned into a high-pressure sales role. The day the management put a sales board up in the Weight Loss Surgery Department was the day I left. I wasn't doing it for 'the sale'; I was doing it to make a difference to people's lives and the day that the patients became numbers was the day my life changed once again.

I had learned a lot over the years working at a high level within the weight loss surgery marketplace. I had made good contacts and easily walked into a management role within another provider. It wasn't long before I realised that this provider was the same as the previous one and saw fat people as their fortune maker. Providers took the money from patients, allowed them to have surgery and then didn't really deliver the aftercare they had promised them at their initial enquiry. I started really thinking about where I wanted to be for the next ten years.

I was still a big BMI (36) so decided to have some more weight-loss surgery as I had started to 'cheat' my band and work against it, which wasn't healthy. After much deliberation I had a part-gastric bypass. This basically means my bowel was re-plumbed so that not only did I have a restrictive procedure with my gastric band I also had a malabsorptive procedure with my gastric bypass. As I only absorbed thirty per cent of what I consumed, I lost another five stone over twelve months and therefore ended up losing fifteen stone in total. When I got down to my target weight I started to get frustrated with my career once again. My marriage also had a big question mark hanging over it. I had married for life but I hadn't married for love. I quickly realised I was not in love with my husband like a wife should be. I loved him like a brother.

At the same time I decided to set up my own weight-loss surgery business to give a certain standard of patient care needed for people who hadn't yet had surgery. Also for those who had surgery elsewhere and desperately needed aftercare. I knew what the journey was like first-hand as I was 'living the dream'. Having surgery had changed my life so much and now I was desperate to help others find the real person they were too. At this point I had lost fifteen stone and wore size ten clothes and that girl who used to be incontinent rarely wore underwear!

I had spent years hiding behind a mask, being the jolly fat girl and always cracking the jokes first... not any more. I wanted people to take me seriously and they saw the 'real' Michelle for the first time. I was finally comfortable in my own skin.

I realised that it wasn't my fault that I had been attacked at thirteen. So I finally let it go and the fat suit came off.

I had a fantastic relationship with a bariatric nurse and the skill set, passion for the patient and strength we had between us was phenomenal, so we started The Weight Loss Surgery Group.

The start up was tough but I had a great business partner in Wendy. She was the gatekeeper of the business clinically and therefore we managed to build up a 'gold standard' service over time. I decided to divorce my husband at the same time – we had grown apart so quickly since I had surgery and we wanted different things out of life. He wanted his dog, fire and slippers whereas I wanted to re-live my teenage years and young adulthood. I wanted to party; I was a size ten for Christ's sake! I needed to start living the life I had missed out on for so long.

The divorce was amicable and I threw myself into the business. Speaking to patients about surgery, seeing them through the process and then, ultimately, seeing the results six months later was so rewarding. I couldn't believe that I was enjoying myself and making a living out of something that had made my life so miserable for such a long time.

The stories you hear from every patient are the same and they break my heart. They pull on me emotionally, especially the young patients. I know exactly what the life they are living is like and also how much of a change is in store for them. I find it very rewarding to be able to make a difference. I will never be financially wealthy from what I do but I will always be rich in spirit.

The Weight Loss Surgery Group was my dream and to see it coming together was an amazing experience. It was totally knackering that first year though. We worked seven days a week, sixteen hours a day to get the business off the ground to ensure we did deliver what we had promised to our patients. We held their hand from their initial enquiry and were with them every step of the way through surgery and beyond.

We also started to offer an aftercare-only service to patients who hadn't had surgery with us but still needed aftercare. This was very challenging as a lot of patients had put themselves through surgery but didn't even know how to use the procedure to lose weight. We saw a lot of patients who thought they had failed with their gastric band or gastric bypass in the first eighteen months. People often think they have failed with surgery, which can be extremely demoralising as it is often a last resort. These patients were demanding but it made us step up a gear. We drew a line in the sand, with their previous experiences on the other side of it, and started from scratch.

It worked and soon the weight loss surgery forums were buzzing about the Weight Loss Surgery Group and we are now working our way up to becoming a market leader in the UK.

As the business started to come together, I began to go out socially and learned the skill of talking to new people. Before surgery I never looked anyone in the eye as I was too ashamed of myself but after surgery, fifteen stone lighter and a size ten, I learned how to party and party I did.

On a night out I met a normal-sized thirty-two-year-old (four years younger than me) and I can only describe him as 'Mr Gorgeous Smorgeous'. He was fantastic; he made me laugh and made me feel comfortable with myself. He wasn't shallow in any way and didn't flinch when I told him I used to be twenty-five stone.

I had promised myself I was going to remain single for at least three years after my marriage ended but Anthony swept me off my feet and, before I knew it, I had moved from the Midlands to Berkshire to be with him. This was love.

Soon after we met something amazing happened – that void in my life was filled – I was pregnant! I was thirty-seven and about to have my first child.

I was shocked, excited and nervous about the baby. I never thought I would ever have children as I had suffered with PCOS. When I first saw my consultant after finding out I was expecting he said that losing so much weight had obviously helped me to conceive.

The pregnancy went well and I had a baby boy on 28 April 2009; he weighed 5 lb 12 oz and is the best thing that has ever happened to me. Becoming a mother is the most phenomenal experience and something that has always been out of my reach until now. I am also the first woman in Britain to have a baby after a gastric bypass and the fitting of a gastric band. We made history.

The pain of all those years, battling with weight issues, the traumatic times I have had, the split from my husband, the issues with food, the fat suit and the demons have all disappeared. These memories have gone back into 'that box' with the biggest padlock on it. Even Houdini wouldn't be able to escape! I now live what I think is a normal life.

I am a mother, a domestic goddess to a gorgeous man and I run a successful business.

However, I do think I was put on this earth for a reason and my mission is not yet complete. I want to make an impact on the obesity epidemic sweeping across the UK. I will do my very best to find time between changing nappies to make that difference.

# DAVID TAIT...

## ... ON HOW THE ABUSE HE SUFFERED AS A CHILD DROVE HIM TO THE TOP OF EVEREST THREE TIMES

*'Over the years I have tried to accomplish many things, some for no other reason than they are simply there to be done. Yet, despite pulling off a few 'spectaculars' such as climbing Everest, I've yet to feel sated. However, I have tried to turn the misfortunes of the past into a vehicle for good by combining my desire for satisfaction into a fundraising tool for the NSPCC (National Society for the Prevention of Cruelty to Children). As a consequence I have summitted Mount Everest three times.'*

Backing onto my grandparents' five-storey town house was a municipal patch of greenery called Deptford Park. It was quite big by inner-London standards. The park boasted a large children's playground with a huge concrete bordered sandpit, a paddling pool, an eighteen-hole putting green and even a full-size cinder athletic track, all set around the edge of a large playing field. Huge, towering oak and horse chestnut trees stood like vast sentries around the whole perimeter.

Tom and Mary Andrews, my mother's parents, lived at 64 Evelyn Street; a road that fast became one of South London's busier arteries. The front of the grimy old house rumbled and shook under the onslaught of passing buses and juggernaut trucks, while the back contrasted vividly; an oasis created by a small garden and incongruous carp pond. Immediately beyond the back garden wall sat the park, a perfect sanctuary from the endless traffic noise.

I loved this house. With its bright yellow front door and religiously polished brass front step, I found the whole environment comforting. Once inside there was a standstill world of lavender perfume, polished brass fireplace ornaments, endless cups of tea and an outside loo. The house stood five-storeys tall, but only the ground and first floors were used.

The creaky wooden stairs, clothed in a deep scarlet carpet and brass rails, led firstly to a small mezzanine floor at the rear of the house where my grandparents slept, before continuing higher. However, the remainder of the house was without any carpets or heating; the doors of the many rooms were kept closed to retain the heat. The first-floor rooms were primarily used for storing old bed frames, semi-broken furniture and discarded light-stands – terrifically exciting caves and caverns just waiting to be repeatedly explored.

The upper reaches of the house became a playground for my young mind, eager and willing to create wonders with my active imagination. With a little help from an old record player and a reclining chair I became 'Scott Tracy', lantern-jawed pilot of Thunderbird One, flying thousands of heroic missions, rescuing hundreds without ever leaving a barren, dusty room on the second floor. The world simply couldn't survive all its dangers without Scott Tracy.

I have nothing but the fondest memories of both my grandparents. Tom was an ex-stevedore, having worked unimaginably hard loading and unloading the huge black barges that once populated the Thames. He had a 'Colonel Sanders' appearance, was immensely strong with the biggest shoulders and hands I have ever seen. Despite his gargantuan paws, he insisted on drinking tea from a dainty china cup and saucer, perplexingly pouring the tea from the cup to the saucer first before sipping. He died in Guy's Hospital in the early 80s, riddled with cancer.

Mary Andrews, my Nan, also known for some mysterious reason as 'Mole' to my grandfather, was everything a grandma should be. Small, round, soft with huge Grandma boobs, and ridiculously generous is how I best remember her. However, no matter how hard I try I cannot remember either her voice or ever having a conversation of note with her. I simply remember her presence there all the time and her being the foundation stone of our family, profoundly appreciated for her roast dinners. She died when I was still at school in the late 70s.

We moved in with my grandparents for three months after completing a return two-week ocean voyage from South Africa. Whilst my parents wandered, house hunting through the interminably depressing suburbs of South London and beyond, my sister and I played all imaginable games in the many deserted, musty rooms of the towering house. Having quickly overcome the tremendous culture shock that a rapid move from the wilds of Africa to the drudgery of London entails, the two of us cautiously ventured onto the open savannah that was Deptford Park. We drifted into a comfortable, simple childhood existence of imaginary heroes, heroines and few, if any, cares.

In the centre of the park stood a small, square, two-room shop that served sweets, ice cream and cups of tea. With two or three iron chair and table ensembles and the ever-present swinging 'Wall's Ice Cream' sign positioned outside, the shop was everything a park shop should be. It was here that my granddad organised my first ever job, my role under the auspices of Mr X, to simply help out by washing cups, sweeping up and stocking the confectionery shelves for £1 per week.

Having been in Africa on a diet rich in fruit rather than chocolate, my sudden introduction to the delights of processed sugar was incredibly seductive. I used to relish opening each new delivery of sweets, revelling in the sight of the orderly packed chocolate bars and rolls of pastels. I dutifully bought sweets using my own hard-earned cash, rather than waiting for hand-outs and quickly developed a favourite indulgence – Fry's Chocolate Cream – a crescent-shaped bar of plain chocolate filled with a mint-cream fondant.

One particular summer's day, I assume a little short of payday, I was in the small store room packing the flimsy cardboard boxes of sweets on the shelves when I discovered an open box of Fry's. The box had split and some of the contents had spilled onto the floor. I remember glancing towards the shopfront and, seeing little risk, I crouched and concealed a bar beneath my shirt. My heartbeat thundered in my ears as I committed this most heinous of crimes. The slick paper wrapping was slippery and the sharp foil ends were needles against my skin.

At that precise moment Mr X suddenly walked into the room. Alarmed, I abruptly stood up, dislodging the chocolate bar from the waistband of my shorts, which fell onto the ground directly between my feet. Horrified, I looked down at the bar, and then immediately up at his face for a reaction. I was at first relieved to see a smile on his lips and what looked like amusement in his magnified, heavily spectacled eyes. 'Put it back,' he said.

Without hesitation I bent down, retrieved the chocolate bar and turned to place it inside the damaged box with the others. As I turned my back I felt a tremendous impact on the right side of my head. I wasn't shocked so much by the actual pain of the blow but instead by the deafening sound it had made within my skull. I don't know whether I was hit with anything other than a flat or clenched hand, but I was stunned by the impact and fell forward. My mouth collided with one of the Meccano-style steel shelves forcing me to bite my tongue.

Suddenly on my hands and knees, I remember seeing a single bright drop of blood fall from my mouth onto the smooth concrete floor and spatter. For a second I stared. I was suddenly half kicked, half pushed from behind, sending me sprawling. A weight, the like of which I had never known, now held me pinned to the ground preventing me from drawing breath. Very close to my right ear I heard through fetid breath, 'Steal from me you little c***?' followed by another hard, stunning blow to my head.

In an instant I was free of the crushing weight but my head was spinning and I was dizzy. I remember keeping my eyes tightly shut as the feeling subsided. The next moment my waistband was grasped from behind and my entire lower half lifted from the floor as my shorts were dragged down. My knees banged painfully against the concrete as he struggled. I had no idea what was happening and was so confused by the wrenching of my clothing that I remember almost trying to move my body in a manner that would make their removal easier – such was my fear of his retribution. Things had to be put right, and I needed to both help and try to please. However, I was raped. It was 1971 and I was nine years old.

I remember so clearly being terrified at the prospect of my parents discovering that I had been caught stealing and even more so by the prospect of police involvement. Even though I was still lying on the floor of the shop, I hadn't for one moment realised what he had done to me was itself a crime. I simply deemed it a punishment for stealing. The whole ordeal had taken only minutes.

He immediately rose to his feet and was almost re-dressed when I turned my head to look behind me. As I got to my feet he handed me a wet cloth from a small corner sink and told me to go into the toilet and clean myself, which I dutifully did. I remember sitting on the harsh wooden toilet seat and defecating involuntarily. The pain was immense and I cried for the first time.

The crying infuriated him and the door was suddenly flung open. There was to be no more crying or my Mum and Dad would hear of it. I stopped immediately. The sight of so much blood on my toilet paper scared me, but I nevertheless cleaned myself and pulled up my shorts. He was waiting just outside when I opened the door. Looking down at me he simply told me to carry on with my jobs. It's quite clear to me now that the last thing he wanted was for me to immediately run home. His caution was rewarded, as a little later I noticed a trickle of blood running down my leg. I returned to the toilet and with his help 'bandaged' myself with a wad of toilet paper.

I was handed three chocolate bars, warned once again, and told to go home. I walked out of the park, along Scawen Road, turned the corner into Evelyn Street, eventually closing the yellow front door of number 64 behind me. I was terrified.

I slipped up the stairs and locked myself in the toilet. As far as I was concerned my downfall was now in my own hands. If my parents discovered blood on my body they would discover the theft and the world would end for me. I would probably be caned.

I remember removing my shorts, and trying to peel away the once sodden, but now dried, wad of bloody toilet paper from between my buttocks. It tore and I cried as quietly as I possibly could. I moistened fresh toilet paper from the wall-roll using water from the toilet and tried to once again clean myself. Apart from the blood between my legs and the bump on my bitten tongue, there wasn't a tell-tale mark on me.

I have little, if any memory of any thoughts or reflections I had at the time. I was too young to make sense of this and was overtly grateful that I wasn't going to suffer at the hands of my father when he discovered his son was a thief – this was my only concern. This was black and white to me. I remember working at the little shop the following day, being relieved that Mr X had indeed kept his word about not telling my parents and also grateful that he chose that day not to touch me. However, this didn't last very long. He knew full well that the terror he had induced in me would keep him safe from discovery. In fact it took time for me to realise that he was in fact enjoying the rape experience; my young mind was unable to understand anything but the excruciating pain I felt. At first I regarded it as a peculiar form of endless 'corporal punishment' for my previous heinous theft but, eventually, after many weeks, I realised that there was a lot more to it. At the time it was nothing I could understand or articulate but enough for me to realise that the act itself was wrong. Slowly, I understood that I in fact had two things that had to remain secret at all costs;

firstly the theft and secondly that I had 'let' this man do things to me that were not right. This was yet another crime, or so I thought.

Eventually, having found a suitable new home, we moved from Deptford to our new semi-detached house in Sanderstead, on the outskirts of Croydon. As far as I can remember, I felt free. Although the abuse hadn't completely ended, it was the beginning of the end. There were a number of visits to my grandparents' house, including one Boxing Day when I couldn't escape his clutches – even in that loveliest of old houses. The desolate, dusty upper rooms sadly served his purposes perfectly.

It eventually ended. I drifted into my teens with a sometimes crowded, confused and cluttered mind. As my general sexual knowledge improved I came to understand fully what I had endured and, to a limited extent, why. It was during these formative years that I felt utterly ashamed of myself and persisted in asking scathing questions. Why had I been so scared? Why didn't I fight? How could I let someone do that to me? All the questions in the world – but I provided myself with very few answers. I was panic-stricken that somehow my secret would be uncovered. Quite how this would happen I wasn't sure; maybe I was now ill as a consequence and I would be forced to confess. Gay jokes that were bandied around at secondary school used to terrify me – did someone know something? Was I gay? My early teenage life was a continual nightmare for me as I slowly learned to come to terms and cope with my experiences.

Looking back now, I can recognise different stages I went through as I tried to deal with what had happened. I progressed from full childhood ignorance to adult understanding, but along the way became depressed and full of hate. On the one hand I could clearly see that my parents were not to blame for the violence inflicted upon me by Mr X. However there were many moments, especially in the early years, when they were my only targets. Parents are there to protect and mine had failed, right?

From self-preservation I developed an ability to ignore things I didn't want to consider. If I hadn't developed this knack, I think at times I would have gone truly mad. However, this same ability caused me to sometimes act in a brutally callous manner – and feel little, if any, remorse. It's only been with the passage of time, and with the gentle help of Vanessa, my wife, that I have been able to shrug off these chains and confront myself.

For far too many years I was forced or maybe chose to use my abuse as a shield; something to hide behind and on which to blame the world's injustices. I also misused my talent for conscienceless action on too many occasions, tossing people and their valuable feelings aside like worthless trinkets. These people deserved much better from me.

However, one pervading feeling that never seems to go away despite the inexorable passage of time is a constant feeling of worthlessness and of feeling second-rate. I know full well I was not to blame but that realisation doesn't seem to help. As a consequence, I think I have always felt compelled to try and excel in the hope that at some point I will be impressed and satisfied with myself.

Over the years I have tried to accomplish many things, some for no other reason than they are simply there to be done. Yet, despite pulling off a few 'spectaculars' such as climbing Everest, I've yet to feel sated. However, I have tried to turn the misfortunes of the past into a vehicle for good by combining my desire for satisfaction into a fundraising tool for the

NSPCC (National Society for the Prevention of Cruelty to Children). As a consequence I have summitted Mount Everest three times.

The first and third summits, in 2005 and 2009, were what could be termed as 'conventional climbs', whereby I first ascended and descended the North (Tibetan) and then the South (Nepalese) side of the mountain. However, in 2007 I hatched a potentially headline-grabbing plan to 'double traverse' the mountain; in essence ascending from the North, descending the South Side and then retracing my steps right back to Tibet in the North, summitting twice in the process.

My motivation in 2005 had been predominantly personal ambition, with a little charitable fundraising thrown in, so I was both surprised and thrilled when I managed to raise £200,000 for the NSPCC. However, the 2007 'double traverse' was conceived in order to facilitate the charity alone. My ego intended to play second fiddle this time. Although I adored the idea of potentially being the first in history to achieve this feat, my intentions were to impress to such an extent that both the charity's profile and coffers would be boosted.

I outlined my ambitious plan to Russell Brice, the owner of Himalayan Experience, the commercial mountaineering operation to whom I owe my 2005 and 2009 summits. I wanted to perform a solo, double traverse, simply employing the infrastructure (tents, food and oxygen etc.) of both 'Himex' in Tibet and 'Adventure Consultants' (another commercial operator run by Guy Cotter) in Nepal.

My desire to climb 'solo' apparently caused Russ, and especially Guy, considerable unease. Although there were minor logistical and major timing issues to overcome, nothing seemed insurmountable. After all, if the plans failed so would

I. It was my problem, no one else's, and I was happy to assume that risk. I can only guess that I was suffering the 'David Sharp legacy'. David had perished, allegedly having been abandoned on the mountain in 2006, in a blaze of cruel publicity, which had erroneously painted the commercial operators in a poor light.

Russ negotiated fees with Adventure Consultants but they simply asked too much for what would likely be only a single week's 'room and board' and half a dozen oxygen bottles. Confronted by this apparent lack of enthusiasm for my project, Russ suggested an alternative. Would I consider climbing as a two-man team with Phurba Tashi Sherpa, one of the most prolific Everest climbers in history and incidentally Russ's right hand-man?

The advantages of doing this were obvious. Firstly, many of the South Side logistical issues would be circumvented, with there no longer being any need for Adventure Consultant Sherpas to be 'on standby' and in appropriately 'safe positions'. Secondly, it was likely that Russ, who would call the shots, would be much less cautious about climbing in dubious weather situations if he had someone with Phurba's experience on the mountain. On reflection it seemed a reasonable proposition to me and one that, given the circumstances and my charitable obligations, I should accept. In the back of my mind however, I was disappointed that I wouldn't be solo but tried to assure myself that despite having Phurba alongside me I would still be the first to double traverse. It was already clear that the 'title' meant more to me than I realised, for reasons that I had yet to own up to.

The expedition members congregated in smoggy Kathmandu towards the very end of March 2007. After a few days checking mountains of equipment at the Yak and Yeti Hotel, we flew to Lhasa and from there began our dusty, bone-shaking road trip across the Tibetan plateau. We rested at progressively higher altitudes before finally arriving at Base Camp (5,200 m), which sits in the shadow of Everest's North Face. The following weeks of acclimatisation climbs and treks urged the necessary blood-chemistry changes but were, on the whole, mundane and unremarkable.

However, I was carrying much more 'luggage' than the average mountaineer. In January 2007 I sent an email to everyone I knew in a further attempt to raise funds for the NSPCC. At the foot of the appeal I disclosed to the world for the first time that I was, or had been, one of the many abused children the charity works so hard to protect. Up until that precise moment, only my wife Vanessa was aware of this. I had decided at that moment that I would no longer hide behind the abuse, and instead of using it as a shield; use it as a weapon for the first time in my life. My intention was that children, teenagers and even adults could hopefully gain strength from my experiences (both good and bad) and fundraising.

By peculiar, but unnerving coincidence, the Discovery Channel chose to send a huge film crew to accompany and record the season's attempts, in the hope of repeating the success of the 2006 *Everest: Beyond the Limit* series. When told that a worldwide audience estimated to be in excess of 100 million people had viewed the 2006 series, I realised that I now had nowhere left to hide.

I had left London on the 29 March 2007, leaving behind my wife Vanessa and four children – Hannah, Oliver, Seth and Ethan. The two elder kids, Hannah and Oliver, had seemed relaxed about my departure but the two younger boys, especially Seth, the eight-year-old, seemed to struggle. It had been hard kissing him goodbye at the front door of our house with him struggling bravely to hold back tears. Vanessa had driven me to Heathrow airport, and stood with me as I checked in. We both knew that the moment when I would step through the departure gate was imminent, so we clung to each other as my huge bags were being processed. Normally so happy and vivacious, she had looked pale and drawn that particular morning, constantly close to tears. I hated to see her distressed, so faced with Hobson's choice I almost rushed to be away. Vanessa knew how hard and lonely the next two months were likely to be, not just coping with the children alone, but also having to steel herself against the possible news of my death. The previous expedition in 2005 had lasted an exceptionally long ten weeks, during which time I had discovered that, compared to being apart from this woman, climbing Everest was easy.

The six tedious weeks of mind-numbing acclimatisation suddenly ended when Russell announced that a suitable weather window was on the horizon that would facilitate our summit push. On 10 May 2007, amidst much fanfare, I left Base Camp. I began my solo trek, via an overnight stop at Interim camp, up the 1,200 vertical and 23,000 horizontal metres to Advanced Base Camp. Russ, my climbing partner, Phurba Tashi Sherpa and I had pored over that morning's weather report, and had concluded that the winds and general weather looked good enough for a summit attempt on maybe the 16 or 17 May.

Phurba is a thirty-six-year-old Nepalese Sherpa, who has worked for and alongside Russell for almost fifteen years. He is clearly Russell's most trusted employee and they appear to have fostered an almost father-son relationship. They walk, talk and act in an almost identical manner, each of them having absorbed and assumed minor traits of the other. Like

Russ, Phurba is a spectacular climber and operator at altitude and is Russell's Sirdar, or head Sherpa. He has summitted Everest a total of sixteen times to date and seems to climb effortlessly. Although at this early point I had yet to discover much about his personality, his reputation preceded him. He is one of the kindest, most modest and unassuming characters you are ever likely to meet. However, on face value, watching him stride purposefully around the camp barking orders to his subordinates, one could mistake his scowl as hostile. But, face-to-face in quiet conversation, it was quickly apparent that he was simply shy.

The speed of the decision to leave Base Camp that same afternoon had caught the Discovery film crew by surprise and now, spurred into action, they asked if they could interview both Phurba and I together prior to my departure. I agreed and set about packing the remainder of my gear whilst they prepared. I sat inside my stifling tent, constantly rethinking the contents of my pack and barrels, eager to avoid errors. All manner of apparently minor and major issues had to be confronted and resolved. I was determined not to let myself suffer through any lack of preparation.

Over previous expeditions I had developed a knack of travelling light, carrying only the lightest of nylon packs. I was constantly amazed by the weight of the huge packs hefted by most of the other climbers. There was no apparent reason for them to have to suffer under this increased and unnecessary burden, but many seemed to simply choose to do so. All the essential equipment such as tents, cooking stoves, sleeping bags and oxygen bottles had already been positioned on the mountain, allowing the Western climbers the luxury of only hauling essentials. However, judging by the size of some of the Western climbers' packs, it appeared as if this had been forgotten. Within my pack, for the forthcoming two-day trek, I carried a Gore-Tex windproof layer, a thick pair of gloves, an extra T-shirt, sun cream, toothbrush and paste, a one litre water bottle, a couple of Snickers bars and my satellite phone. As long as I took the time and care to hydrate properly in advance of my departure I wouldn't need any more than a further litre of liquid en route.

Up until the precise moment I started walking I had found myself a little nervous and apprehensive. There was nothing I could point at that explained this. The feeling had seemingly come from nowhere and had honestly surprised me. Literally minutes after my first steps I once again felt calm and ordered – so much so that I remember looking up at the mountain, now shrouded in early afternoon cloud, and smiling to myself. I glanced down at my feet, wondering once again if they were capable of transporting me these many miles, over so many ancient rocks.

Ten minutes after leaving camp my path led into the shallow ravine created by the surrounding mountains and the edge of the Rongbuk Glacier. I glanced back for one last look at a now distant Base Camp. The moraine rose to my right about 30 m, while the mountains to my left rose 5–600 m. Directly ahead, 22 km away, sat a brooding Everest.

I woke in Camp One (North Col) on 13 May, at 7,000 m. I had slept well, despite the cold, swaddled in my down-suit and two sleeping bags. My bladder, however, was desperate to get some attention, so unzipping my jacket I removed the warm half-full pee bottle.

I had to keep it close during the freezing nights, as if the contents froze, it would simply mean more weight for me to carry until it eventually thawed. Also, straight after my midnight pees, it was actually quite pleasant hugging the relatively hot bottle – one's thoughts didn't linger too much over the contents. I wrestled with my many layers of clothing and eventually negotiated myself into a suitable position that allowed me to add to the contents. All this was done blind, still lying flat but simply employing a gentle twist of the hips and the use of a carefully placed finger within the neck of the bottle, to prevent any ugly overflow.

Suitably relieved, I glanced at my watch – 5.30 a.m., but by now it was thankfully getting light. I reached for my iPod and relaxed. The day ahead was going to be more than tough and I wanted to be ready. I didn't want to start the day with a headache, but that was what I had. I immediately swallowed three ibuprofen; the only drug that seemed to combat my swelling brain stem. I then slowly drank my remaining unfrozen water. I lay back, closed my eyes and listened to Till Brönner, some of the mellowest jazz I have within my collection.

The ibuprofen cocktail I had swallowed engineered a dreamless hour-long sleep, but Phurba, knocking on my tent urging me to my feet, woke me. A little embarrassed and surprised by the lost hour, I quickly packed away my still frosty equipment, eventually unzipping the tent front, only to be blinded by the intense sun. It was a quite beautiful day; the snow was new, soft and brilliant white. At least a foot of fresh powder had covered my previous evening's tracks and it took considerable effort to clear myself an exit. Before long though, I was standing in front of my tent, marvelling at the stunning view and fending off the early-morning hypoxic dizziness. Resigning myself to the inevitable nausea, I began the breathless trudge towards the mess tent, where I found a very composed Phurba chatting on the radio in Nepalese to his Sherpa colleagues. He was talking to a party of perhaps a dozen high altitude Himex Sherpas, who were now only minutes from the Col, having left Advanced Base Camp that same morning at 4 a.m. These guys were destined to climb the North Ridge alongside the two of us. It was odd to think that to these tireless individuals, today, and frankly every other day, was just another day at the office. As Phurba and I laboured ever higher, I was constantly reminded that I was surrounded by men who could all probably summit three times a season and think nothing of it, other than relishing in the much needed funds it brought their families. I was starting to feel a little awkward.

Water was already boiling on our two small gas stoves and I wondered just how long Phurba had been awake. I sat down, stared at the various packets of food dotted around the tent and tried to coerce some enthusiasm from my reluctant taste buds. However, nothing seemed to work, so I contented myself with a combination of digestive biscuits and Alpen bars, all washed down with lukewarm water. It was a struggle to say the least, but not to eat would certainly result in my grinding to a halt. I forced myself to chew, at the same time wriggling my semi-numb toes, encouraging them back to life. As Phurba spoke in rapid Nepalese, I glanced around the mess tent, reflecting on the fact that this would be the last time I would ever have to endure this place – at least on an ascent. One of the sad facts of life on the mountain is that one doesn't appreciate the wonder of the things around you as you experience them. You generally feel either so focused or so ill that nature's wonders or simply a moment of reflection is often denied. I had pledged to myself that I would, despite my inevitably negative frame of mind, force myself to store these unique days away in some deep recess of my mind. More often than not, the simple task of retrieving a camera from a pocket to record a view can seem just too much hard work.

Phurba's radio suddenly resonated to the sounds of Russ's voice. After a brief greeting and enquiry as to our general health, he advised us that the weather outlook hadn't changed and that our fifteenth summit attempt still looked OK. We were both very relieved, as the thought of having to descend only to try again later in the month obviously didn't appeal. Minutes later we heard the high-altitude Sherpa party arrive and Phurba signed off in order to meet and organise them. I finished my splendid breakfast, donned my crampons and carefully exited the tent.

The Sherpas were milling around loading their packs for the next leg of their climb with a back-breaking combination of oxygen bottles and Therm-a-Rest mattresses. I stood and watched in pure admiration as each of these relatively diminutive men loaded three oxygen cylinders and two mats each into what were already bulging packs. Then without a moment's hesitation they slung these huge weights onto their backs, sometimes not even bothering to secure the load-spreading waist belt, and began the formidable march higher to Camp Two.

'This is embarrassing,' I thought, and I actually found myself avoiding eye contact. I had gone to extreme lengths to pare my load down to its bare minimum, even going so far as refusing Discovery's request to carry a 3 kg head-mounted camera, just in case it compromised me at higher altitudes. As I reflected on this, I watched Phurba refill his pack. Phurba's food bag alone probably weighed the same as my entire pack. In addition to this, he carried the camera equipment, water, a change of clothes, two oxygen masks, the Himex radio, sun cream and a 15 m length of rope. This was all I had noticed, but there was probably a lot more.

The Sherpas were silently streaming out of camp, trudging towards the beginning of the North Ridge, so to distract myself from these thoughts I decided to join them. The weather was as perfect and the wind as still as it had been on the acclimatisation climb weeks earlier. This inevitably meant that before very long I was dramatically overheating. I decided to wait a short time just to be sure that I wasn't mistaken about the negligible wind, as the sudden appearance of a breeze can alter your temperature from very hot and sweating to cold and shivering in a matter of seconds. Unfortunately for me the breeze didn't appear, and within 150 m I had stopped to unzip my down-suit and tie the top half around my waist. Unfortunately I find these stifling conditions debilitating; I'm a person who much prefers colder climates for exertion.

Three and a half hours later, I crested the last ridge before Camp Two (7,500 m) and paradoxically found myself happy that I was continuing without spending another fruitless and uncomfortable night here. Camp Two is set into the snow, just beneath the start of Everest's first exposed, ancient rock. It's a barren and often brutally windswept place, with little going for it. So rather than peeling off left towards the Himex tents, I continued upwards, skirting to the right around a large rocky outcrop, the same location of a disastrous pee attempt in 2005. I had then just hurriedly left Camp Two before suddenly noticing that perhaps it would have been super-smart to have emptied my bladder before doing so. However, I was now trussed up in my climbing harness and dressed in my thick down-suit.

Going for a pee with all this gear on is never easy, but just to make things interesting I also had to contend with a freezing, swirling gale. Having managed to negotiate myself free of my clothing, I turned my back to the wind and relaxed. However, the wind wasn't consistent, and the adjacent rocks created a cruel vortex around me, unfortunately returning my 'stream' and essentially soaking me from head to foot. Luckily, though, the temperature and wind-chill combined to freeze the pee instantly, leaving me totally encrusted with thousands of bright yellow frozen droplets. Absurdly, I remember glancing around to make sure no one had seen me.

I stopped for a short breather before taking to the rocks. I glanced back down the slope behind me. I was being followed by one of the Himex Sherpas who had been slowly closing up on me over the hours. He was older than the rest, probably closer to forty. I noticed that he was wearing a Discovery Channel camera, bolted to the side of a lightweight, scarlet cycling helmet and also boasting a metre-long aerial protruding from his oversized pack. When I had first noticed him behind me many hours earlier I had thought it was Phurba. Now, little more than twenty metres behind me it was clear who it was. We nodded briefly at each other and sat together in silence for a while before moving off. I led up the rocky face, simply following the blue nylon ropes these same Sherpas had laid in the days earlier. I wondered to myself just how many times my mute climbing companion had been through these exact rocks this season alone.

Making slow but certain progress, we edged our now haphazard way through the rock, snow and boulders. The gradient was erratic, giving only a few moments of respite and with every step the air seemed to be getting thinner. I stopped and for a moment I leaned my forehead against the rocks and was suddenly mesmerised by the rock itself. The stone appeared as charcoal sometimes does; fractured, and apparently about to crumble. With my gloved hand I nudged the surface but nothing dislodged. I suddenly saw the rock as ancient wood and remembered the brittle appearance of logs after a fire. The rock appeared very similar indeed.

Dragging myself back to the present, I hauled myself forward, noticing that the purple-clothed climber ahead of me had pulled further away. The rope wound its way randomly up the face, anchored only intermittently. I was getting tired now but I had noticed that the climber ahead had apparently disappeared from view, so I surmised, optimistically, that he had reached his tent and ducked out of sight.

Once again the collection of Himex tents had been set at the upper limits of what was perceived to be Camp Three, but I eventually struggled onto the minor plateau at approximately 1.30 p.m. – six hours after leaving the Col. I was weary and eager to escape the wind. I looked around at the small band of Sherpas casually organising the camp. Phurba had mentioned to me just prior to departure that our tent would be the first on the right as I entered the camp. However, as I made my way towards it, I was directed towards another. Not in any mood to question this instruction, I squeezed through the designated tent's front aperture, turned and sat with my back against a huge mound of equipment. Clearly I was in the wrong tent but, at that moment, it didn't seem crucially important. I zipped the door closed, lay back and immediately fell asleep as my body rapidly warmed.

In what seemed like moments, I was rudely shaken awake. Phurba had arrived, discovered me asleep amongst the stores and ordered me up and into our own tent. A full hour had passed whilst I was blissfully unconscious. Dragging myself to my feet I tiptoed, crampon-less, across the ice to the adjacent tent and made myself at home.

Before very long snow was melting on our miniature stove and I was sipping a welcome cup-a-soup. We spent the remainder of the afternoon entombed within the tent, eating, drinking and making the occasional radio call to both Russ and Phurba's South Side contacts. It was warm, almost uncomfortably so, as the wind died and the intense sun beat remorselessly down upon our tent. I lay, for the most part, flat on my back, either listening to my iPod, or Phurba, who seemed to pray endlessly. He would take a small book of scripture from a colourful, embroidered pouch that he hung around his neck and recite prayers for hours. I found it strangely comforting and marvelled yet again at his dedication. I once asked him about his faith and he sang its virtues and mentioned with obvious pride that his brother was a practicing monk, who had begun his service when he was just five years old. I had noticed what an active part Phurba had taken in the Pooja (religious blessing) many weeks ago back in Base Camp, and so it was clear that his faith was dear to him.

He showed me a small collection of letters that his Nepalese colleagues had charged him with carrying and delivering to relatives living on the South Side of the mountain. Together with this mail, he had a huge number of rupees, which he was excited about gifting to the local monastery. It turned out that this was a gift from Russell – I wasn't surprised. We continued to gently discuss his beliefs, expanding the conversation to include our respective families and domestic lives. I was amazed to hear that not one person within Phurba's family knew he was attempting to traverse. He simply planned to show up and surprise them.

As the sun drifted lower, so did the temperature and I readied myself for sleep. I was comfortable, warm and not hungry. I forced myself to drink half a litre of water, emptied my bladder, put my earplugs in, texted home and then drifted off to sleep; little thought was given to the fact that I was balancing on a ledge at 7,800 m.

'Shit – no wind,' I thought to myself as I prised my eyes open in Camp Three. It was 14 May. It was light and the tent was already aglow with the early morning sunshine. The temperature at 6.30 a.m. was still low, but not uncomfortably so. In another time and place this pleasant fact would likely be greeted with cheer, but to me, climbing in the heat was far more debilitating than the cold. I glanced across as Phurba sat up, turned on the radio and immediately fumbled for a lighter to ignite the gas stove. I had nothing to do except negotiate safe passage for my urine to the pee bottle, lie back and stare at the ceiling of the tent.

Even though we were only due to climb a further 500 vertical metres to Camp Four on that day, the fact that we were scheduled to depart for the summit at 11 p.m. meant in all likelihood we wouldn't sleep again until the evening of 15 May. When, if successful, we would be safe at the South Side Camp Two (6,400 m). That would make for a gruelling thirty-six hour day, tough at the best of times, but particularly nasty whilst hauling yourself over Everest above 8,000 m, short of food, liquid and oxygen. With water now boiling and the sun drenching the tent, I mustered the energy to sit up and organise my pack for the next leg. As Phurba poured Alpen and boiling water into two bowls, I opened a packet of biscuits, made some jasmine tea and sat in silence, chewing. Eating was less of a challenge this morning, something for which I was more than grateful. Once finished we carefully organised our multi-layered clothing, before squeezing into our harnesses.

Phurba left the tent first and we both stood outside for a long moment before securing our crampons. With my pack lying on the ground I took the opportunity to briefly film us at Camp Three. The view was once again stunning; the sun was brilliant, the sky deep blue and we gazed down on the surrounding peaks jutting through a blanket of clouds. It was a beautiful vista and on that morning, owing to the lack of wind, very peaceful. I glanced up the mountain, my eyes following the blue rope, and noticed that the Sherpas who had accompanied us yesterday were already well into the day's climb. I could see a number of orange Himex down-suits dotted up the rock and scree slope. Now I had to follow.

I squeezed my oversized padded arms through the shoulder straps and, taking care not to tangle my oxygen line, manoeuvred it onto my back. Comfortable, I dragged the black elastic straps of the face mask over my head and tightened them in place. Once everything was secure and I was under at least the vague apprehension that I could feel a little benefit from the flowing oxygen, I edged over to the fixed line and clipped in. I didn't use my ascender because the gradient wasn't acute at this point, and with a relatively slack rope it's a huge inconvenience. So with simply a karabiner linking me to the blue nylon, I started my trudge up the hill. I guessed, somewhat hopefully, that I might complete the climb and wander into Camp Four in about four hours.

The first few metres are always a struggle as your body suddenly screams in protest at the sudden suffocating exertion. Luckily an unobstructed path suddenly developed and the gradient dropped to perhaps thirty degrees, allowing me to settle into a slow, steady rhythm. Phurba had already pulled ahead of me by twenty-five metres but frustratingly the distance gradually widened.

The scree slope became jumbled rock, demanding significantly more effort. The trail narrowed and the exposure magnified. However, the guide rope negates most, if not all, worries you have with regard to falling into the abyss. The climb is simply hours of small groups of steps, interspersed with equally numerous rests.

This tedious routine continues unabated for hours on end, the only entertainment being the thoughts in your head or the music in your ears.

After about ninety minutes, I stopped for a brief rest and water break, turned, sat and retrieved my camera from my pack. Looking back down the incline I could still see Camp Three clearly and was as surprised as I remember being in 2005 that despite all the effort the camp still appeared so close. Gazing out over the surrounding peaks, I noticed that apart from the summit of Everest, nothing within sight was higher than I was right now. I glanced down for the first time at my altimeter and the numbers confirmed that I had indeed crossed into the so-called 'death-zone'. It's a very dramatic, tabloid term, but in reality you don't even notice. '8,000 m' is simply a nice round, romantic number.

I noticed two other isolated climbers perhaps 150 m behind me and decided to get going once again. Turning to look further up the trail I became aware that I could no longer see Phurba, or any of the other Sherpas for that matter. I wasn't sure if they had maintained a fearsome pace today or I had simply been lagging behind, but this comparison between us once again gnawed at my conscience.

I could never dream of equalling this man, let alone beating him. I was fully aware that what we were attempting was not meant to be a competition between the two of us, but it was becoming increasingly obvious that the disparity between our relative performances was too great to be ignored. This contrast is something that is deliberately overlooked by climbers of all nationalities whilst climbing on Everest and I presume other Himalayan peaks. When I climbed in 2005, I was grateful to the Sherpas for all the effort they had put in, but I was so focused on achieving my personal dream, at almost any cost, that I excluded them from my thought-processes to all intents and purposes. This 'record' attempt had given me a totally different perspective on my relative contribution.

Hauling myself to my feet, I trudged on, staring for the most part at my boots. The sun beat down and I felt myself start to slowly broil within the down-suit. Undoing every available zipped vent, I tried to encourage a relieving cool airflow around my body, but it was to little avail. The gradient over perhaps the last two hours of the climb seemed a constant forty-five/fifty degrees and for this period I employed the jumar (ascending device), for no other reason than to be able to sit back in my harness and occasionally rest.

The terrain was generally snow, but regularly altered to sheet ice. This meant that you had to orientate your feet outwards, effectively climbing on the inside edge of your boots. I found, and have always found, this terribly uncomfortable and tiring – no doubt I'm not alone in thinking this and was grateful whenever the surface softened, so I could re-angle myself. The last thirty to forty-five minute climb up the final slope into Camp Four was tougher than I had expected. I had been debating within my hypoxic mind the merits of what I had set out to achieve for many hours now, and I had started to convince myself that my efforts were futile.

If I had been alone in my quest and climbing solo, which was my original plan, my athletic performance over the term of the traverse wouldn't have mattered in the slightest. There would be no comparisons made in my mind or others. However, Phurba was standing in direct contrast to my ability and the more I contemplated asking him to essentially 'move aside' for me in order that I summit first, the more I began to feel like a horse's arse.

By the time I staggered into Camp Four, I was pretty downbeat. I trudged to the entrance of the tent and Phurba, obviously without knowing he was making me feel even smaller, crawled out, knelt and removed my crampons for me. It was a simple, kind gesture, but one that further tortured me. I crawled into the tent, arranged my gear and lay back, but not before Phurba handed me a hot tea. He sat cross-legged, having shed both his boots and down-suit and frankly waited on me, making sure I was comfortable before starting to cook.

Over the course of that stiflingly hot afternoon in the tent together, I battled my demons. I had reached a crucial point where I had convinced myself of the futility of following this man up, down and back over this mountain. Having originally attempted to traverse solo, this wasn't what I had envisaged many months before. I reached for my sat-phone and firstly called Russ at Base Camp and then Vanessa at home. I presume I came over more than a little hypoxic and emotional, as I found it very hard to articulate quite what I was feeling. Nothing was going to stop me summitting a second time that night, but I no longer saw much merit in continuing down the South Side, preferring instead to leave Phurba to do it and rightfully enjoy the plaudits. I can't quite remember what Vanessa said, but it worked, as by the end of the conversation the idea of summitting and then descending, as I had in 2005, back down the North Side, wasn't an option any longer.

More than once I tried to explain how I was feeling to Phurba, saying that I didn't feel justified in claiming such a 'title' whilst accompanied by someone as accomplished as he. Either he didn't understand or he chose to appear not to, because all he would say was, 'Decide on the summit'.

A little later we ate, the two of us sharing some boil-in-the-bag vegetable curry and a selection of biscuits. We continued to boil water, drink and refill our bottles methodically as we gradually lost the light and were enveloped by cold. My spirits had soared simply because I had postponed making tough decisions until once on the summit. Having changed into my 'summit socks', a brand new pair reserved especially for the long day ahead, I re-laced my inner boots, set my battery-operated warmers on level two of three and relaxed. There was nothing to do now except wait and attempt to sleep. Phurba continued to sit cross-legged rocking gently as he recited his endless prayers, forcing me to resort to my iPod for some distraction. He read his prayer book by the light given off from his headlamp, which totally banished the prospect of slumber.

The dark, cold hours dragged by in Camp Four. Then, the familiar crunch of crampon boots could be heard. Eerie, ghost-like shadows thrown over our tent by the first of tonight's summit climbers roused the two of us from our silent contemplation. With headlamps illuminated and the now icy interior of the tent glistening, we started our preparation. It was 10:15 p.m. and we had decided not to leave the tent until 11 p.m. – quite why Phurba had insisted on leaving so late was a mystery to me as my instincts had told me to leave earlier, and with every subsequent gasping climber that passed our tent I felt progressively more vindicated.

I felt the tension building within me like a coiled spring and tried, in vain, to relax. I felt as eager to get on with it as I had done two years before – I wanted to leave the tent at once to reassure myself that yes, I could still move my legs at this altitude and the previous six hours of enforced, tedious inactivity had done nothing to thwart my summit attempt.

With everything now in place, we squeezed from the tent and out into the night. It was an exhilarating time. I stood for a moment watching Phurba adjust his pack, and looked back down the incline I had struggled up during those hot daylight hours. Amidst the total blackness below was a shaky line of glowing headlamps edging their way higher. I turned to look above and noticed the same, only now I was just able to make out each individual, seemingly hanging in space, as the small halogen lights occasionally reflected off the snowy, vertical rocks.

We set off with me in the lead. Force breathing myself and concentrating on taking two full breathes for every step; I found the going surprisingly easy. I felt as strong as an ox, even turning to Phurba to ask if my pace was sufficient. He replied that perhaps it was even a little too fast, which surprised me. Soon the easy snow steps ended and we were confronted with our first rock wall. I clipped my jumar in, took three or four deep breaths and scrambled up – my crampons skidding on the scarred rocks for purchase. During these short, exhausting bursts you have a paradoxical tendency to hold your breath. People do it all the time at sea level under exertion but rarely realise. However, at altitude and already starved of precious oxygen, any interruption to an established breathing pattern is immediately noticeable and regrettable. At times like this your lungs feel as if they are about to burst, as you desperately suck the oxygen into your pain-wracked body. Before long we had caught up with a couple of other climbers. From behind me Phurba called out to the Sherpa of the pair, who suddenly stopped and turned to look at us. 'Go past,' said Phurba, and I surged into the small gap they had allowed. As it was a relatively warm night of perhaps fifteen degrees, no one found it necessary to wear protective goggles. As I passed the two climbers I glanced up at them, noticing the relaxed and smiling face of the Sherpa and by contrast the already pained expression of his Japanese client's face whom he was escorting to the top of the world. At times the channel through the rock we were all negotiating en route to the ridgeline narrowed into almost 'chimney' dimensions but, other than being a draw on the lungs, it wasn't hard to climb.

Scooting around numerous other small parties, we cleared the exit-cracks and stood atop the ridgeline ninety minutes after leaving Camp Four. I might be mistaken, but I'm sure this same climb took me three hours in 2005, but that's now ancient history. Either way, my perception of our relative speed was a tremendous boost to my confidence. Without any need for hesitation and without any desire to search for evidence of 'Green Boots', the fluorescent-clad climber who perished on this spot many years ago, we continued on through the deep snow. The alarmingly large number of headlamps that preceded us along the ridge disturbed me. Were we likely to suffer in the predicted traffic jam at both the first and second step, as the Himex team had done in 2006?

Maintaining quite a thrilling pace, Phurba and I soon flanked a group of Japanese climbers being directed from the rear by their Sherpa. Very quickly Phurba began his ruthless negotiating process and we were soon let through to continue on our way. The ridgeline has no noticeable gradient to speak of; it undulates a little and is occasionally quite exposed, with brutally sheer drops to the right. However, the benefit of climbing at night is that your precarious perch is masked – you could be climbing Box Hill in Surrey on a winter's day, with trees and green fields beyond the wall of darkness. Even when orientating a powerful headlamp into the abyss that you know is there, the light is devoured by the blackness, revealing nothing.

I enjoyed climbing in the dark. I don't know if it's simply the novelty that seems to force the passage of time, but I was surprised by how quickly we got to the 'first step'. However, a line of patient climbers waited for their turn to mount the wall, as if waiting for the remotest bus in the world. In what appeared to be slow motion, climbers began the exhausting scramble through the jumble of huge boulders that form this natural 'climbing-wall'. Ropes from previous years littered the route and cluttered the pitons (a climbing aid hammered into a rock face). I stood and watched as people struggled like exhausted glow worms up the face, resting annoyingly often.

At last it was my turn and trying to use my legs, as opposed to my arms, as much as possible, I entered this rocky bottleneck. Finding secure purchase for my feet wasn't difficult and with a slow-moving person ahead of me, I had ample time for rest as we edged higher. I was able to look around and reflect about where I was and what I was doing. It seemed strange to think that here I was climbing the first step on Everest at 1 a.m., at maybe 8,600 m, while at home it was only 8 p.m. and the kids were probably still playing in the garden. It was a confusing thought.

Before long we were standing on the plateau at the head of the first step, feeling energised and ready for the next stage. Ahead of us the ridgeline disappeared into blackness, occasionally dotted with the glow of lamps. We trudged on, our pace urgent and determined, clipping and unclipping as each length of rope was negotiated.

In the distance I could see the line of lamps orientate sharply upwards and I knew this to be the much larger second step. We rounded a jagged rocky outcrop, our crampons screeching against the stone, and were confronted with a horrifyingly long line of very slow-moving climbers. I turned and looked imploringly at Phurba who was resting, hands on knees. He unclipped himself from the rope, reaching past me to re-secure himself to the line and stepped gingerly past. He started talking to the man at the rear of this line of perhaps a dozen climbers but he was a Westerner and chose not to respond. Phurba tried once more to engage him, trying in vain to force some understanding from him – but none was forthcoming.

'Go past?' Phurba asked, turning back to me. I was nodding vigorously, already sucking in sweet lungfuls of oxygen in anticipation. We both unclipped and, climbing a little higher than the climbers ahead, ignored the beaten track and broke our own trail through the knee-deep snow as we passed them. At one point, in order to overtake as many as we could in the available space, we actually broke into a brief jog. I still remember the startled looks on these pedestrian mountaineers as we both bounded by. Once safely past and clipped to the line once again we both laughed and then continued.

Out of the darkness loomed Mushroom Rock, a rock so named for its uncanny resemblance to a potato, I assume, around which congregated a small bunch of resting climbers. I was overjoyed to see so many generous souls willing to be overtaken before the second step. I glanced down at one man who seemed in distress; his breath rasping loudly and I remember catching his eye as I drifted past.

My mind briefly flashed back to the sad demise of David Sharp, the solo English climber who had perished so publicly on Everest in 2006. His parents and brother had accompanied Himex this season to Base Camp, presumably in an attempt to find some peace from their grief. In that instant I asked myself, would I, if asked, be prepared to forgo my summit to help this unknown man down to safety? I didn't allow myself to ponder, knowing only too well how hard it would be to do the 'right' thing and turn your back on your dream.

Leaving Mushroom Rock behind us, we laboured forward and before very long we had joined a huge queue of climbers patiently waiting their turn to do battle with the second step. When we arrived, at perhaps 3 a.m., there were approximately thirty people ahead of us, all standing nose to tail and shuffling forward at less than a snail's pace. I watched Phurba bobbing his head left and right, talking to the Sherpa ahead, but I sensed that any attempt to bully our way further up the line would be futile. Phurba obviously came to the same conclusion, as he suddenly became as still as the rest of us, idly watching the other climbers inch their way up and past this vast obelisk. In the silence I could hear Phurba praying, the chant now surprisingly comforting. I did wonder for a moment if he had started praying because he had proprietary knowledge of some forthcoming disaster, but I laughed it off.

We stood for perhaps an hour in this extraordinary queue at the top of the world, alone with our thoughts, gently moving from one foot to the other to keep warm. A slight breeze had arisen and I started to feel my fingers chill. I clenched my hands into balls within my mitts, trying to exercise the blood flow and again reflected just how miserable it must have been twelve months before, with significantly lower temperatures and far harsher winds.

My moment had come and I stepped forward. Having watched many flounder during their first steps, as they tried to find a convincing grip on the early slippery rocks, I elected to use the 'bull in a china shop' approach. It seemed to me that the tentative, considered approach had more often than not ended in failure. Now panicked and embarrassed, climbers appeared to finally lunge at the face in desperation. So lunge I did and, in a few lung-searing moments, had sufficient purchase with my crampons to relieve my shoulders, which were supporting this maximum effort, dangling as I was from the various old ropes.

With the first awkward boulder passed and my breath recovered, the remainder of the lower section of the step was easily traversed and ahead loomed the upper section of the second step. We shuffled a metre or two through the snow and fell once again into line. We watched the now way too familiar leading climbers mount and climb the famous ladder. Phurba and his band of supermen had fixed this ladder alongside the deficient but equally famous Chinese Ladder in 2004. A few weeks earlier whilst fixing ropes to the summit, Phurba had also re-engineered the ladders in an attempt to alleviate some of the bottleneck issues, particularly on the second step.

I laughed to myself once again. No one around us realised that they were standing alongside the guy who had actually put the ladder there in the first place! I wondered if Phurba ever pondered this fact. One by one we climbed the cold aluminium, our steel crampons screeching against the rungs, before finally stretching out to grasp the safety of the solid rock as we reached the top.

We clipped in once again and continued. I wasn't in the slightest bit tired, and was relishing every moment. Phurba stopped to answer a radio call from Russ, advising him that we were now at the top of the second step. Around us I noticed the sky had slightly lightened – my favourite moment was close. Unimpeded now by any noticeable obstacle, save the altitude, we made short work of the relatively even surface that terminated at the unimpressive looking third and final step.

Still maintaining our relatively impressive pace, I wondered just how quickly we would have covered the ground to the summit from Camp Four if we had been alone on the mountain. At that moment I thought we could have done it in half the time, if it hadn't been for the traffic jams. The third step is an uninspiring pile of rocks; far less impressive than the first two and, far from being a challenge, feels more of an inconvenience. However, there is no way around the lump, so we scrambled over it, becoming part of a now closely packed chain of climbers all conscious of the fact that they were within an hour of reaching their goal.

Beyond the third step lies the foot of the snow pyramid, and it was at this point in 2005 that I stepped over a fallen climber – someone who had died only a few days before. He lay on his back with his legs hooked above him over some rocks – almost as if he had been sitting in a chair that had fallen over backwards. Unfortunately the line had run over his waxy skin and empty expression. Despite admittedly being tempted, I fought the impulse to photograph him, fearful that this would bring bad luck or bad karma. I stepped over him and continued.

He remains there, but covered to all intents and purposes by the deep snow, only minor parts of his red suit jutting through. Most wouldn't have known he was there. I turned and looked back at the rising sun behind me. It was and will always be one of the most beautiful things I have ever seen. The curvature of the earth is vivid and all the surrounding peaks glisten and shine. Separating them were the deep, cold and still-dark valleys, but even in this early light I could see the white tongues of jagged glaciers. These very glaciers I had laboured along a matter of days ago. The one lingering impression I had was of the extreme clarity of the view. Later I was to describe this phenomenon as the difference one experiences when switching from ordinary analogue to high-definition television – the difference is mesmerising; something you didn't think possible.

The snake of multicoloured climbers inched their way up the unstable slope, the snow was deep and crumbly in places but hard and icy in others. Halfway up there was a natural cleft in the snow, perhaps two or three feet high. As I heaved myself up and over it the snow collapsed, making the cleft even harder to negotiate for the unfortunates behind me. But by then I was up. If the climber behind and beneath me had had any breath or energy to spare, I'm sure abuse would have been hurled in my direction.

Two steps and rest, two steps and rest until at last we both crested the small brow of the summit pyramid. Now on horizontal ground, we deviated to the right and onto a thin rocky ledge. We were now traversing alongside the 'dihedral' and this is where one gets a true sense of exposure. The darkness is gone, the sun is brilliant and you can no longer be under any illusions as to exactly where you are. Twenty or thirty metres along this thin, horizontal rock ledge, a natural aperture in the rocks inviting you yet higher suddenly appears above.

However, we were once again halted by another queue of exhausted climbers waiting their turn to scale these final slippery rocks. I glanced downwards to my right and noticed yet another body, one that hadn't been there when I summitted in 2005, lying perhaps ten metres beneath the ledge. I got the impression that the body had perhaps been placed there, as its posture was 'organised' – the face and all skin was covered. I then remembered that Phurba and his team had also been employed to deal with all the residual dead bodies during their 'window-dressing'.

Relying on the fixed ropes to hold my entire body weight and concentrating on not holding my breath, I clattered up the fifteen-metre rock face. During this short ascent I suddenly felt extraordinarily tired. Every step and every movement that passed reduced me to frantic gasping. I knew from experience that the summit was close, but I was still alarmed at my sudden inexplicable decline.

At the top of the rock the snow slope continued for perhaps thirty metres to another small ridgeline – the summit still concealing itself at a shallow thirty-degree gradient. Phurba had walked ahead of me by fifteen metres and stopped to look back. Without exaggeration it took every ounce of effort I could muster in order to cover these few metres and join him. My legs simply refused to move and my lungs seemed to stop functioning. I felt ridiculous, having to stop for ten seconds after every single step, even when no further apart from Phurba than two paltry metres. Eventually I got to him and he immediately turned me around to check my oxygen.

I had run out and it hadn't once occurred to me that this had happened. I dropped to my knees as he fumbled within my pack, changing over my regulator to my remaining fresh bottle and removing the old.

The difference, once he turned on the flow, was simply amazing. It was only at that point that I truly appreciated firstly just how much benefit we get from the supplementary oxygen, but also just how strong those climbers are who summit this mountain without it. Feeling reborn, I followed Phurba over the small ridge and for the first time saw the summit, thirty metres ahead and perhaps a further ten metres higher. I stood for a moment and gazed in wonder at a sight I had first seen with my climbing partner Richard Staite on 4 June 2005 – and it hadn't changed a bit.

In little more than ten minutes we stood side by side, bizarrely waiting for a 'turn' on the crowded summit. There were maybe ten men huddled together atop the small dome pinnacle. Some sat, some stood and others waved flags while their colleagues photographed and filmed the moment for posterity. In a few moments we had our chance and, scurrying around and approaching from the southern aspect found our space, we embraced and shook hands. Phurba called Russ on the radio to report in.

'Big boss, big boss,' Phurba yelled into the microphone.

'Go ahead,' answered Russ.

'David and I are now on the summit,' he said.

'Congratulations to you Phurba Tashi on your twelfth summit, and you David on your second,' crackled Russ from far below, his formality making me suspect he was being filmed. We had made it at last. It was 6:15 a.m., 15 May 2007.

During our endless descent down in Nepal, I kept asking myself over and over how I was going to be able to ask, if not instruct, this most humble and gracious of men to make way for me just so that I could claim a mountaineering title. He had no dislikeable or selfish traits with which I could discern and excuse myself. He seemed to have tireless energy, patience and faith, never once having shown even the slightest hint of temper or exasperation. He either had the will power and control of a Greek God or just perhaps, in this most disappointing of worlds, he was the real McCoy. The westernised cynic in me kept looking for a chink in this man's moral armour, but despite being tested to the ultimate degree he never once faltered.

I saw myself, in my minds eye, ten metres shy of our return on the second summit, drawing to a halt and requesting that I now go first. As I conjured up the somewhat vile image in my now completely focused mind, I saw myself unable to look into his eyes. I realised that what I was going to have to do, in order to achieve a world-first, was rob someone. It's true that there was very little chance of Phurba being there in the first place had I not conceived or financed the attempt, but this offered me little if any succour.

My reservations were far more fundamental, and were in fact now part of my core. I had decided to take on this challenge in order to prove to myself that I could do something notable; something that would make me feel special and not 'second-rate'. My childhood experiences had left me damaged in more than just physical ways. I felt Deptford Park had moved me to the periphery of the human race, often unable to enjoy even the simplest of pleasures others take for granted, such as simple, friendly conversation. I feared contact, especially throughout my early teenage years, fearing parties or the company of my peers – fears that still linger today. I loathed my terror. So, in an attempt to gain a grasp on my own self-esteem, I set about trying to impress myself. I felt that the only way I could raise myself in my own eyes was to achieve what appeared to be the impossible. No matter what it entailed.

But here I was about to finish our first traverse and soon begin our second, knowing full well that, even if I did succeed, my 'claim' to the so-called title would be hollow. Phurba could beat anyone I had met in my meagre mountaineering career to the summit of Mount Everest, yet some forty-five-year-old Hedge Fund Manager was about to claim it all for himself, for no other reason than that he 'paid' for it. Later, but not before walking through the strangest collection of ice pinnacles, almost with the appearance of a frozen sea, we clambered up a short rock moraine and into Camp Two, 6,400 m – the South Side Advanced Base Camp. It was 6.30 p.m. and we had been descending for twelve straight hours, climbing for a total of twenty-six and awake for an eyelid-challenging thirty-six.

All the members of Adventure Consultants, climbers and Sherpas alike, came out and welcomed us with applause and cheers. It was a lovely moment, one I was grateful for and one that I will never forget. I shook hands with many, eventually being introduced to Guy Cotter, the head of Adventure Consultants, who congratulated me on being the first Brit and Westerner (subsequently confirmed) to traverse Everest from north to south. I was amazed, but also quite elated by the unexpected news, so much so that I, at that precise moment, knew that I wouldn't attempt a return traverse.

The little shop still sits in the centre of Deptford Park, surrounded by those beautiful trees. Generations have wandered, played, slept and loved on that small oasis during the thirty-five-odd years since the day those protective trees turned their backs on me. Countless children have bought their sweets over the worn wooden counter and perhaps countless more have worked inside for a little pocket money, as I did.

I have sometimes wondered if there is any scar left on the soul of the building or whether, much like in a Stephen King novel, a disturbance can be felt by those more sensitive. Was it possible that nature was so affronted by the violence that some psychic spoor was left to mark the spot?

It would be easy to believe that one is so special that nature or perhaps even God might have noticed, objected and perhaps made some amends. But in reality it's more likely to have been missed. The earth didn't shake; the sky didn't blacken, shot through with lightening bolts. In fact nothing happened at all.

Well, maybe one thing happened. From that day I seemed to lose my ability to be happy and to relish even the most joyful of moments. The physical trauma healed as my body renewed and grew to manhood, but on my mind was inflicted the greater injury. Despite time's recognised ability to heal, there is a part of me that is still as raw as it was when I was a child. The feeling isn't quite as all embracing now as it was then but, when I allow myself reflection, I feel myself burn afresh.

I have combated this open wound by developing, through constant practise, the ability to literally 'turn off' my emotions. If I choose not to feel, I won't feel; it's as simple as that. There have been many times when this questionable talent has saved my life, but equally there have been too many occasions when it has destroyed the lives of others.

The cruel punishment I meted out to both my parents for crimes they had no idea they committed, in fact didn't commit, arguably resulted in their eventual deaths.

I only have myself to blame for these callous actions, but I feel at least a little justified in apportioning some of the blame to Deptford Park. It's only as I've got older that I have been able to confront the many crimes of my past, both committed by and against me.

Yet my struggle for self-respect goes on. For reasons that I cannot explain I still feel somehow responsible for my childhood demise, so much so that I'm plagued with a lingering, but deep-seated, self-loathing. Every ounce of intelligence and common sense screams at me that I was innocent and unable to withstand the assault, but nevertheless I am cursed with doubt.

The passing years have been dotted with sometimes impressive and sometimes ridiculous attempts to bolster myself. Many challenges have been assumed, met and conquered, but despite brief positive fillips there have been little, if any, long-term benefits. My success in summitting Everest in 2005 lifted me, somewhat appropriately, higher than I have ever been, but the intoxicating feeling of superiority was transitory at best. However, it had an addictive quality.

I conceived of the 'double traverse' in late 2005. After performing due diligence, I discovered to my delight that it had never been attempted and, confident in my own ability, committed myself to the challenge. Maybe such a feat and becoming the 'first person' to do something would do such wonders for my self-esteem that I would at last feel unburdened.

The reluctance of Everest's commercial operators to be associated with my planned solo attempt left me with few options but to climb with Phurba. However, in accepting to climb as a pair I knew I was storing away a future problem. Despite discussing my reservations with a number of trusted people I, for the most part, pigeon-holed the issue and, true to form, refused to confront it. Once on Everest, and force-fed with Phurba's superiority, I had nowhere to hide.

I had a simple choice to make. Cross the mountain first, asking Phurba to move aside and hide from the reality each time I looked in the mirror, or face up to the fact that decency should take priority. After so many years of introspection, I knew that I had reached a moment of truth. Was I so pathetic as to need a make-believe title to feel human again? Had I learned nothing over the years? I could once again employ my long-nurtured talent and refuse to think about the reality – after all I'd had enough practise. I was about to bully the most gentle of men to let me pass, whilst ironically holding a NSPCC flag.

I can't deny being proud of the titles I did earn from traversing the mountain. They were hard won, but legitimately so. My ego is grateful for the small mercies. However, I know that I made the correct decision to return home. It was time for me to stop putting myself first and to stop hiding behind the shield of abuse. I had originally come to the mountain with the intention of using the abuse as a weapon, publicly admitting everything to my friends and perhaps the world through the Discovery Programme in order to further the charities cause.

What I had almost done was show the world that, despite being well intentioned, I had learned nothing from my torments. In front of the world I had almost demonstrated that despite my humiliation I still had the ability to humiliate others. I am glad I stopped short. Maybe there is a challenge out there that will lift me to a dreamy height from which I will never fall, but I doubt it. I think the self-loathing will accompany me to the grave but, as time passes, will be less likely to drive me there.

I hope that both children and adults, either previously abused or not, will read or view what I have done and take heart. When your mind, body and soul are violated to such a degree you are confronted with a fork in the road; to the right lies a possible future, admittedly with problems, but a future nonetheless; to the left lies despair, misery and a possible premature death. Over my life I have been confronted with moments of profound choice, when, tormented to my soul's core, I have had to choose between life and death. Somehow death has always seemed a little too easy and I have turned away.

Life, especially carrying such a secret, is unlikely to be perfect, but it can still be pretty close. When you are standing in front of that fork, alone, ashamed and hollow, it's easy to permanently close your eyes. You must, at that precise moment, choose to fight back and not immerse yourself in misery. Once free of your tormentor, life is still there to be lived and will be altered by your ordeal only as much as you allow it to be.

# CRAIG GREEN...

## ... ON BEATING HIS NEAR-FATAL ADDICTION TO HEROIN

*'But I carried on as normal and those profound moments of clarity soon gave way to a sense of distant regret, overshadowed by my first thought upon waking; where was my next hit coming from?'*

Anyone who has successfully beaten a heroin addiction has my absolute respect. There is no doubt in my mind that climbing out of my addiction to the drug is the hardest thing I have ever done and will remain so until I die.

I had a fairly normal upbringing; I wasn't abused or bullied as a child. I don't really have any of the cliché reasons or excuses a lot of addicts cite when trying to explain or justify themselves. I slipped into the lifestyle by an ugly combination of chance, naivety, curiosity and, perhaps most dangerous of all, fearlessness.

At school I was a quiet kid. I didn't have many friends, but the ones I did have were close. I had a friend called Sam. Our parents were friends so our relationship grew from circumstance. When our parents wanted to drink or have barbecues, my sister, Sam and myself would always end up forced into some room together to play.

Sam and I were best friends from day one. We were born two days apart. Growing up with him though, I always knew our friendship would not have existed had it not been for our parents as he wasn't exactly the nicest kid. We used to play-fight and he always used to go too far. He was certainly rougher than I was, in every sense of the word.

We went to secondary school together, where our differences were further highlighted by our choice of companions. His crowd was at the opposite end of the spectrum to my group of friends. But this did not stop us remaining close. We were friends throughout school and as we both began to mature, so did our relationship.

He stopped being such a brat and I lightened up a bit. We found a balance. I would describe our behaviour as relatively normal during school. We made a habit of smoking behind the school bike sheds, which actually housed no bikes but rather broken tables and old hockey sticks. It was still a great place to smoke, though.

He would steal tobacco from his dad and claim he had bought it himself and, despite being about fourteen and looking about twelve, most of the other kids believed him. We would have roll-ups at lunchtime for no other reason than because we knew we were not allowed. I believe this is a fairly normal trait in teenagers, regardless of cultural background. The desire to rebel is probably built into us and almost certainly has an evolutionary explanation. If I am honest, I don't remember actually enjoying those grotty dry rollies in the slightest but I certainly enjoyed the kudos that I thought they brought with them.

CRAIG GREEN

Later in school we began smoking cannabis together and
again, at my school, this wasn't a big deal. Lots of kids were
doing it, especially the older college-age ones. The only thing
that differed was our ages. We seemed to be the only ones
smoking in our year. Which brought further kudos; I was
certainly very cool, despite the fact I was only doing it to
appear so.

We would play truant and end up drinking Sam's dad's beers
and smoking his tobacco. I felt sorry for the poor guy – he
must have thought he was going mad because his beers and
tobacco would deplete at an alarming rate. I am sure he had
his suspicions. Drinking soon became our main pastime. We
would drink at the most inappropriate times. We were around
sixteen years old and I started to notice that I wasn't drinking
and smoking to be cool any more, I was genuinely having fun.
In the same way I had only spent time with Sam because of
our parents, I started to really like him. We had such a laugh
together; we really were best friends.

We were remarkably resourceful when it came to procuring
alcohol. There was a shop not far from my home that was
owned by a sweet old lady. Sam used to pretend she would
serve him alcohol, but only on the proviso that he was on
his own. I knew for a fact that not only was Sam very short
and in no way did he look old enough but he didn't have any
money, either. At the time I didn't give it much thought but I
am fairly sure he was stealing all the booze. If he stole beer
without batting an eyelid from his own father he probably
wouldn't have too many qualms about pinching a bit from
the corner shop.

We would drink at the weekend and get up to all sorts of
trouble. Our parents would be fed some lies about us playing
scrabble at one of our friends' houses, or something equally

as absurd. This would allow us to sit around in the park, on a bench, near some bins or anywhere that we could drink cheap booze and smoke roll-ups.

Other mutual friends would come and go but Sam and I would always be there for each other. We would always choose spending time mucking about with each other over virtually anything else.

In college I calmed down a bit. I would still drink heavily at the weekend, which wasn't unusual at that age. In fact, not drinking heavily at the weekends is far more unusual. It was at college that I met Kelly; she was in my tutor group and she was the only person who made an effort to talk to me on the first day. Everyone else seemed to already have friends and even though she seemed busy talking to hers, she still approached me and struck up a conversation. I chose to be a bit of a loner but I must still have looked a little desperate sometimes, sitting alone, quietly in the corner. But she spoke to me, not out of pity but simply because she is a lovely person. Love at first sight is impossible, but I think I came close to believing it for a while that day.

We became a couple and although Sam never vocalised or expressed it, I knew there was jealousy. We had been virtually inseparable for years and now this new girl had arrived and stolen me away. We all got along fine and would spend time together, but the presence of a female will always tone down the behaviour of two men. This perhaps was a good thing but I could tell Sam was always yearning to get outrageously drunk and climb on people's cars, or something just as stupid.

Sam dropped out of college after a heated argument with his tutor. He did PE and took a football dispute a little too far. During a fight he ended up hospitalising another student. Sam argued that the injuries he caused to the other boy, the worst of which was a broken finger, were superficial and all the fuss was blown out of proportion. The staff at the college didn't seem to agree and when threatening him with disciplinary action he stormed out – never to return.

This meant that I didn't see him half as much. My relationship with Kelly became stronger and I think I was happy. Kelly was no stranger to recreational drinking, drug-taking and general rock and roll, which meant that even without Sam I was still smoking and drinking perhaps more than the average. But again, just like with Sam, I was enjoying myself. Your youth really is the best time of your life, when responsibilities are pretty much nonexistent and you can live carefree. It wasn't too much of a problem behaving like I did during that time in my life. When you are young, reckless behaviour is fine. I enjoyed those years more than I knew at the time.

Sam worked for a while on building sites for one of his relatives but after his consistent rebellious nature and lack of respect for authority emerged he was again kicking his heels.

After college Kelly and I went to university, sadly different universities. This meant we broke up. We drifted apart very quickly and although we both thought we would remain close we stopped the phone calls within the month. I wasn't that bothered by this at the time – our relationship had come to an amicable end. It felt organic that we should go our separate ways but I really was in love with her. She was incredible. I think back now over our time together, the fun we had and the times we spent laughing. We were together for nearly two years and yet I simply can't remember having a genuine argument with her. That is not some kind of blind memory of our love but rather testament to the strength of our relationship; I don't think we did fight. I will always have fond memories of her.

In life I only truly understood two things, which were maths and painting. A strange combination, I know, but nevertheless those were my specialties. I took mathematics at university but struggled with the work, ironically not because it was too hard, but because I wasn't being challenged. It sounds arrogant but I was 'smarter' than nearly everyone else and none of them knew how to have fun. I mean proper fun; the kind of fun I had with Sam.

I dropped out of university before the first term was over. I was back home and I felt lost. I had no drive; there was nothing I really wanted to do. Everyone else had gone off perusing something or other. But nothing was for me; the only thing I knew how to do really well was have fun, so that's what I did.

I had a job in a bar, which paid me just enough money to drink almost every day. Within the year I was working at two different pubs and was drinking most waking hours. Once again, I was best friends with Sam. He was still unemployed but was making as much, if not more, money than I was, selling pot and cocaine.

I helped him with his 'business' – my maths came in handy when bagging and dividing ever-larger amounts of drugs. I moved into a horrible little bedsit with him, which really only had one bedroom that had been crudely divided into two by someone that probably called themselves a builder, but who was almost certainly a con artist at heart. Seriously, it was a half-built plaster wall that you couldn't touch or else it would crumble. It was a disgusting little place but a great base to run things from.

Again, I was having fun. When you are that age you're not considered an alcoholic; you just drink a lot. I had done cocaine a couple of times at college parties but never regularly. Both

Sam and I were fully hooked on coke before too long. This wasn't actually as problematic as it sounds because we could afford it; we were comfortably funding our own habit, which I would still describe as recreational. I think it is quite normal for middle-range drug dealers – like we were – to sniff all the profit. We never considered ourselves drug dealers, or addicts for that matter, because we were selling to 'friends'. We were just selling to lots of friends who were only friends with us because of the drugs we sold to them. I grasped this quite quickly but Sam still persisted in trying to befriend our clients.

I was regularly finding myself at 'parties', a term which I use very loosely. They usually consisted of vomiting and passing out in furniture-free flats that belonged to someone who we vaguely knew. I was fully aware that my only connection with my 'friends' was the drug habit we shared.

My family life had become virtually non-existent. I occasionally saw my parents and would receive the odd phone call from my dad. My sister moved to the USA in her mid-twenties, when I was still in school. I had always loved her; she was by far my favourite member of our family. I got a phone call from my dad to let me know that she had killed herself and that she was going to be flown home to be buried in this country. This was a fairly large amount of hassle for my parents but something they insisted on doing. I thought it was a bit pointless as I knew she wouldn't have wanted anyone to have made all the commotion they did. Even in her note she specifically requested that no one made a fuss over her death, which I imagine she did tongue in cheek as she knew my mother would insist on a large funeral with extended family in attendance.

Apparently, she had become depressed after splitting with her boyfriend and had started drinking – I guess it runs in the family! I was sad at the time but as I hadn't seen her for years it didn't bother me too much. The sister I remember wouldn't have wanted me to worry, so I didn't.

I had drifted away from my family during that time but I knew that her death had hit my mother hard. She explained that all she wanted was the whole family to give her a good send off. Then she would be able to mourn and finally let go. That level of sentimentality isn't my cup of tea, but I knew how much it meant to my mother.

On the day of the funeral, I consciously chose to sell a huge amount of dope and go out drinking instead of attending. I know my sister wouldn't have cared but I was fully aware that it would break my mother's heart. All she wanted was for me to be there, that's all, and I didn't have to say or do anything, just be there. It would have taken less than an hour to show my face; that's all. One hour. I wasn't pressured or forced not to go, I chose not to. If I think about that decision at night I can't sleep, even now. If I wake up in the night and remember that day, I won't get back to sleep. I am yet to apologise to my mother. I don't know if there is anything I can say that will make what I did any less painful for her.

I had essentially cut ties with my family. My parents weren't stupid; they knew what I was up to, and the only blood relative I cared about had moved away and killed herself. I truly had nothing to care about. I would consider myself a 'junky' at this point in my life, even before I had touched heroin.

I was off my face on all sorts most of the time. When I wasn't drunk I was stoned. I was taking cocaine daily, routinely. I still worked at both jobs but I was never really there. I was more like a zombie. I didn't care about anything. Nothing fazed me and nothing bothered me. I was going nowhere, slowly.

I remember finding Sam collapsed on the stairs that lead up to our flat. I came home from the pub quite late one night and he was lying in the most uncomfortable-looking position I had ever seen. Finding Sam unconscious was not an unusual thing but he appeared more unconscious than I had ever seen him – not at all responsive. He was dead to the world. I made sure he was still breathing before dragging him inside and leaving him on the sofa. Our sofa had actually been sawn in half one drunken evening. I couldn't tell you why, but both halves were pushed together. It looked as though it had a great story behind it, which I wish I could remember!

The next evening he was in the same clothes and was lying in a similar position on the sofa. I had been to work and popped round to my parents' house to have a cold conversation with them about nothing in particular; the weather, work or anything else that wasn't about my lifestyle – the elephant in the room. I didn't know if Sam had moved or had been there since the night before.

Sam was on heroin. I didn't know this at the time because although we lived together, we didn't really talk to each other. Obviously, we spoke but we never talked about what we were doing. That is something I can grasp now, when we were going through all of this we would reminisce about our past experiences. Always talking about 'that time we…' meant we never had to worry about the present or how terrible the route we were on really was.

Not long after that we were at one of our 'parties' where people were taking heroin. I had been around people doing heroin before; it wasn't shocking to me. Sam sat down and instinctively began shooting up. Looking back I should have been shocked by this, but I wasn't. This was Sam; I don't think he had shocked me since primary school when he left dog faeces on the teacher's chair. I wish I could say that story is not true but sadly, and quite hilariously, it is.

It is important to remember that I was not under any pressure to join in and take heroin. I didn't feel forced, I didn't feel as if I should. Dealing drugs is a business like any other. Dealers are looking to sell drugs to make money. If there is a demand – whether they create it or it occurs naturally – they are happy. So in a sense by immersing myself in the environment I suppose I was under a subconscious pressure to join in but I genuinely believe there to be no actual malice behind my partaking; it was entirely my decision.

Why do people take recreational drugs? To feel good. Much the same reason people do most things. I had been drinking to feel good, taking drugs to feel good and having carefree sex to feel good. I was as self-centred as it is possible to be; all I wanted to do was have fun and consequences did not factor into my decisions.

I know now that I was addicted to alcohol and cocaine during this period but at the time I believed I could stop. I knew I could stop. I was just having a laugh. I was young and invincible. I feared nothing.

I didn't even know the man's first name, just his bizarre nickname, but I trusted him to prepare an injection for me. It was like nothing I had ever felt before. I was the embodiment of absolute comfort.

I had explored some crazy highs with various drugs in my time but this was something completely different. It is hard to describe but imagine when you wake up in the night and happen to be lying in an incredibly comfortable position, you are just the right temperature and you drift off to sleep again. The moment when you are fully conscious and aware of your comfort times about a million. The feeling was nothing short of awesome... however, Newton's third law states: 'for every action there is an equal and opposite reaction.'

I had spoken with addicts before. People who had been hooked on crack cocaine and heroin. I heard them describe the addiction, the feeling they got days after a binge, the powerful desire for more and how utterly terrible it was to go without. That didn't apply to me because I knew I was getting more heroin long before any withdrawal symptoms appeared.

I was back at this guy's house shooting up a second time long before my body gave me the urges. I didn't give a shit about anything. I remember consciously thinking, 'What's the worst that could happen?' I rationally came to the conclusion that the good far outweighed the bad. I have never been more wrong about anything in my life.

That was it. That moment, that decision changed my life more than I could ever have known at the time. Before long, I was doing heroin more often than lots of long-term users I knew. I had money and nothing else to do. I will never know how easily I could have stopped in those early days because I never really gave myself a proper chance to live without it for any significant length of time.

Heroin isn't like other drugs. It is addictive in every sense of the word. During prolonged use it causes chemical and molecular changes to the brain. To put it simply: unlike most drugs, it literally changes your mind. Also a tolerance can be built up fairly quickly, meaning larger doses need to be taken for similar results – this increases exponentially over time – meaning that eventually you need to take heroin to feel normal. The good becomes normal and the bad becomes absolutely fucking dreadful. It dehydrates you by both affecting your water intake (you drink less because you're off your face) and your liquid absorption. There is a huge list of side effects – ranging from feeling a little under the weather to dying. I could have listed them then; I knew the risks. I had been told all about the drug. Ignorance is neither an excuse nor an explanation for my behaviour.

During this period I started to treat food as a fuel. I would just eat slices of bread to give me enough energy to get from A to B. Over time my weight loss and muscle fatigue started catching people's attention. I quit one job, where I did daytime shifts. My boss at the other bar I was working at was concerned for me, not angry that I was too weak to do a lot of the tasks. There were benches outside that had to be brought into the garden at night. He asked me one evening to move them and I said I couldn't. He didn't care that I wasn't doing my job properly; he was just worried for me.

Eventually he fired me but not because I couldn't do my job, but because he thought I was ill and was keeping it secret. He knew I drank lots and did drugs but I think he thought I was terminally ill, which I kind of was in a very self-inflicted way. His heart was in the right place but without a regular income I was in lots of trouble. He didn't realise how damaging firing me would actually be.

Sam had been slacking for a while. His only income was dealing drugs, which he was now too lazy to actually do. What kind of drug dealer can't be bothered to deal drugs? Heroin addiction isn't ideal when you've got money but when you haven't it is absolutely terrible. Things got bad very quickly.

We were both fully dependent on heroin. The man we got it from was reliable; he always had lots and would regularly tick us drugs (because he knew we were good for the money). Now we weren't, neither of us had an income, but still we had a very expensive habit to upkeep.

Again we became very resourceful. Just like our cunning ways when we were young, we would find ways to get odd bits of cash here and there. Our dealer got a bit tougher with us when we racked up quite a debt with him. But we still got by, just.

The relationship between a heroin dealer and his customers is a very bizarre one. On one hand, what he is doing is terrible; he is truly evil. But on the other hand he was saving us from the most awful prospect; not having heroin. He was exploiting us, but we were literally begging him to do so.

Occasionally Sam would turn up with a load of cash and would insist I didn't ask him where he got it. He would say, 'I'm not proud of myself, but look at all this!' Sam has to do something very bad to feel shame; it doesn't even bear thinking about how he got a lot of that money.

One trip to our dealer's house will stick with me for life. We turned up at about midnight one evening and we walked into a war zone. There were about ten people, rushing around and panicking in the tiny garden behind his place. We went to see what was happening. It was absolute chaos; the air was buzzing with panic. Lying on the floor, flat on her back was a girl. She was dead. I didn't have to check her pulse; she was obviously dead. Junkies die all the time for a lot of different reasons. People associate heroin with its addictive qualities but often forget that it is a powerful intravenous substance and, if you get it wrong, it can be fatal. Sticking any substance directly into your bloodstream is certainly a risky thing to do.

I vaguely knew the girl. She had been in the pub where I used to work but on the floor she looked like a mummy. Her skin was so tight around her bones. I don't know if she was just really skinny or if it was an effect of whatever had killed her but she looked disgusting. Like something from a cheap horror film; it was a ghastly sight. Everyone was arguing and panicking. I heard people suggesting she be taken and left somewhere or delivered to her family house. I couldn't begin to fathom the horror of discovering someone in her state on your doorstep, especially not a loved one. I prayed that, whatever had happened to her that night, no matter what awful circumstances had led to her death, she didn't end up back home looking like that. We left straight away; we didn't need the hassle of it all.

It worried me that she was lying on her back. I wondered if the simple action of placing her in the recovery position might have saved her life. It chilled me to think that she died because no one knew what to do or, worse, no one cared. I think that was the first moment that I had serious doubts about my lifestyle. This was a very dark business.

The man who sold us drugs ended up in prison not long after that. The police found him with a car full (yes, full) of drugs; the kind of quantities that make even veteran officers gasp. I never found out the exact amounts but I think we're talking in kilos and in double figures. But supply and demand means that another drug dealer will happily take his place. That's how it works. That's how prohibition does not work.

We plodded on, getting bits of money here and there. We were borrowing it, stealing it and all sorts. We were relatively clever thieves, but thieves we were. Sam had some very dodgy relatives who would buy stolen goods without batting an eyelid. If they didn't want something they usually knew someone who did. Everyone knows 'a bloke from the pub' who will pay money for something.

We broke into big homes to steal TVs, stereos and anything else that we could sell for even the smallest sum of money. We would break into building sites at night to steal power tools, mixers or basically anything shiny. I am quite a moral person; I did feel bad about what we were doing. But it was a cold fact that we needed money for our heroin. Bottom line. I would insist we stole from large sites so I could console myself with the fact that all of it was insured, and it was just the large corporate insurance companies that were losing out. I pretended there was no real victim in it all. I knew deep down it was wrong, but I also knew there were degrees of wrong.

Once we came extremely close to selling some items back to the people we stole them from. This wasn't nearly as funny as it sounds. It makes sense when you think about it; they had asked around for anyone who had a cement mixer for sale on the cheap because theirs had gone walkabout. We arranged to meet them through Sam's cousin. We were smart enough to always meet away from our place. We knew we were breaking the law.

We pulled up in a car park in the van we had borrowed from Sam's cousin. I spotted two big rough-looking characters leaning against a white van. We were moments away from approaching them when I recognised the symbol on their van. Thank God I did. If they'd had a look at the mixer, they would have certainly recognised it as theirs and I can't imagine they would have been too happy about that.

We had a few close calls like that. Sam got arrested a couple of times when he would go out alone on one of his 'missions' as he used to call them. Which I expect probably consisted of mugging people near cash machines but I never wanted to know. I could give him the benefit of the doubt and absolve myself of the guilt if I didn't ask.

When you need some heroin your body really lets you know. Overwhelming nausea and a feeling of discomfort takes control. It is horrible what happens. I would seem to get a lot more ill than Sam did. It would play with my emotions, too; I would be all over the place. I knew that one day I was going to quit the drug but I kept it as a distant prospect – I couldn't face the idea of going for any length of time without it.

During a very eventful evening I fell down some concrete stairs and ended up in hospital. I came round in a bed, topless and very confused. I hadn't seen myself properly in a mirror for a long time and I was genuinely shocked when I looked across the ward and saw myself looking back. I looked terrible. I had lost so much weight, I had dirty stubble and my skin was an absolute mess. A gorgeous nurse came and spoke to me as I drifted in and out of consciousness. I only had a broken foot, so she must have known there was more wrong with me than my physical injuries.

Again, like so many others, she seemed genuinely concerned. She wasn't judging me or looking down at me like some people did. She just wanted to help me. I met a lot of people like this. Obviously, there were people who wouldn't be quite as kind; 'junky scum' seemed to be thrown around on occasion, for example. But I seemed to come into contact with a lot more people who seemed to care than those who didn't. People were genuinely worried about me even though I was a person they didn't know. I couldn't understand it. I didn't care about anything or anyone and I couldn't grasp why these people were worried for me. What was in it for them?

Like always, I didn't care what she had to say. I got out and headed home on crutches. The day after I was in hospital I had dinner at my parents' house. Something that they insisted on from time to time, probably not to see me but just to make sure I actually ate something. I was a mess during this time. My parents were concerned. It was obvious that I was on heroin, but it was as if that word didn't exist in their vocabulary.

They would probe at the topic but it would never be openly discussed. They would just suggest I saw someone about my problems. A vague attempt at a solution, but they were right. I did need to do something but I was yet to completely agree with them.

It was a Sunday evening and I insisted on walking home by myself, despite the crutches and the distance. Walking was always nice and distracting. When I had to walk somewhere, it was like bonus time. I could think.

When I got home, Sam was sprawled on the floor outside the front door. He had been beaten up. As I have said, finding Sam unconscious was never a shock to me. This time, though, it was. He had been beaten so badly that his right eye looked as though it was missing or completely destroyed. I had never seen violence like it in my life.

I dragged him inside, which wasn't easy, and put him on the sofa – his half, I didn't want blood on mine. I was always scared to let anyone but Sam come into our flat. It became a bit of an obsession. I was ashamed of how we lived and I was terrified I would get arrested. Nothing to do with fear of jail or any of the normal reasons people don't want to go to prison, but simply because I wouldn't be able to find any smack. I knew they would force me to take methadone to wean me off, which was a prospect that scared me more than death. For those reasons I tried to treat Sam's wounds myself rather than calling an ambulance.

Blood was pouring out of him like a tap. It took me about ten minutes to pluck up the courage to call an ambulance, by which time I was in tears and could barely speak. He was in such a state. He was missing teeth and his right eye was so badly swollen it didn't look real. His skin was stretched almost to bursting point.

I was back in hospital, less than forty-eight hours after I had left. This time Sam wasn't going to get away with the excuse, 'I fell down some steps.' The police were going to be involved and this scared me.

Sam came round and couldn't explain who had beaten him up, or why. All we knew was that they were kind enough to drop him off at home. He had probably tried to mug the wrong person or had stolen something he shouldn't have. I remember a policeman speaking to me about it all. The good-looking nurse who treated my foot was in the ward. He told her to leave. He put his notepad down and took his jacket off. At first I thought he was going to beat me up but he just wanted to talk to me as a man, not as a police officer. He spoke to me about a girl that went to school with his son. She died recently from a bad batch of heroin. She died one evening not long ago in a back garden not far from the hospital – small world. I didn't tell him that I had actually seen this dead girl. He was trying to scare me, or shock me, or get through to me somehow, but it wasn't working.

I still wasn't convinced that I needed to think seriously about sorting my life out; that specific moment was yet to come. My relationship with Sam became very different. Despite losing sight in one eye, he recovered from his injuries with minor scars. We carried on as we had been. Stealing, mugging, conning or whatever needed to be done to get some cash and ultimately some drugs. We bought from a couple of different dealers, one of which was not a nice man at all – he was an awful man in fact.

I never wanted to speak with him. Sam always made contact and arranged meetings. But steadily I ended up being associated with this terrible individual. I had always trusted Sam more than anyone else, which is not to say I properly trusted him – because I didn't. I just felt I could rely on him over others, but I was wrong.

I remember going to meet this man at his house, which was surprisingly nice considering his profession. Sam had sent me to collect some drugs that we were planning to sell. Sam still did the odd favour here and there for this man. He would sell the odd bit of cocaine or act as a middleman for certain deals. I had no idea of the logistics of this particular arrangement but I was there representing Sam.

I walked straight into the building as instructed. There were a few extremely rough-looking men and one heavily pregnant woman sitting around in the living room. The room was full of smoke and the smell of booze was in the air. It was a terrible environment to say the least. Sam had lied to me about why I was there. This man came into the room and instructed me to sit down. He was trying to intimidate me and it was working. He told the woman to leave the house. It was just me, him and five of his friends.

I was pinned down and threatened with a knife. As they restrained me he kept saying he was going to make it quick and that I should hold still so as not to make a mess. It was terrifying. He didn't kill me and had not planned to at all. He was just looking to scare me, which he did. It turned out that Sam owed the man £400. That is all; just £400. Now it was both Sam's debt and mine. I had just had my life threatened over £400. What on earth was going on?

Sam disappeared for almost a week. I ended up borrowing some money and paying this debt back. Upon Sam's return he refused to tell me where he had been, making no effort to pay me back and, worst of all, he would not apologise.

At the age of about fourteen Sam stole money from another student at school. I can't even remember the amount now but it was around a fiver. The cash was taken from the kid's bag. Sam and I were outside a nearby classroom after misbehaving. We were doing our science work in the corridor. I saw Sam take the money and I stayed silent. The following day we were interrogated over the crime. The evidence was stacked against us, but neither of us would admit it. I blindly denied the incident, whereas Sam said I had taken the money. I can think of more examples of Sam being a terrible friend than I can of him being a great one. He would climb over anyone, even me, to better himself in even the smallest of ways.

He had stitched me up one too many times. I was done with him. We were simply not friends any more. This had been the case for a long time. I started spending a lot of time just out and about, sitting in the street, sleeping on benches and generally just appearing to be a tramp. I was still doing heroin and I was still doing things that I am not proud of to get cash.

I remember standing in a cafe one sunny Saturday. I was buying a drink. Standing in the queue I saw a child who must have been about five years old. He was staring at me. Probably because I was wearing disgusting clothes and I looked like a zombie. Or perhaps because that is just what children do. He was looking at me with a neutral expression; there was nothing in his eyes apart from a shred of concern. Even this child, a five-year-old, could see that there was something very wrong with me. He can't have known what, but he could tell that I wasn't all right. Clutching his mum's skirt, he stared up at me with innocence, curiosity and, most significantly, concern.

Parting ways with Sam, seeing that poor dead girl, choosing to miss my sister's funeral and now this bizarre prolonged eye contact with a child were all moments that were beginning to stick with me. What was I doing? I had completely lost myself. I wasn't a person and I wasn't really living. There were so many points where I would think, 'This is ridiculous and I have to sort myself out.' But I carried on as normal and those profound moments of clarity soon gave way to a sense of distant regret, overshadowed by my first thought upon waking; where was my next hit coming from?

The most significant of these moments hit me hard. I was rarely at home, because I couldn't stand to be around Sam. I had nothing to do besides take and then find means to acquire more heroin. I spent a lot of time slumped in the street. I looked like a tramp so I was treated like one. People gave me odd bits of change although I never once asked for any. I was ill at this point, I always had cold-like symptoms, but now I was very ill. I was malnourished and I looked truly awful.

Sitting there on the street one day half-awake, trying to keep my head up, someone caught my eye. There was a beautiful redhead walking up the street towards me. I knew her. It was Kelly. She used to be dark blonde but had dyed her hair red. She looked just as beautiful as I remembered her. I hadn't seen her for years but every feeling I had flooded back to me as she walked along the pavement, just going about her business. I am not religious in the slightest but she was glowing like an angel. She was clearly happy and was smartly dressed. She looked so clean and gorgeous.

I hadn't taken notice of anyone for a long time. Looking back I properly lost my ability to communicate with people when I was in that state. I realise now that I never really made eye contact with anyone. It sounds strange but I didn't think of people as people. I never thought of a person as a human, just like I was. People were just things. They were these strange lumps that I could get money or heroin from, nothing else. I didn't know that at the time, but looking back that is exactly how I was. Even my parents never got my attention. I didn't know them and they didn't know me. Sam was the closest thing to a genuine person in my life and I hated him.

But here was Kelly, looking nothing short of incredible, the embodiment of beauty. I hadn't felt 'good' for a while. I felt a chemically induced replica of good from heroin quite often. But actual emotions or naturally formed smiles were alien to me. There was something left in me though, all hope wasn't gone. Walking up the street was this beautiful girl, who had once loved me. I don't know if I was on the outside, but on the inside I was smiling. I was grinning like a schoolboy.

Whilst sitting on the pavement, I looked up at her with puppy dog eyes. She didn't know how much seeing her had meant; she didn't know how profound her being there was for me. Then the worst thing I could imagine happened. As she passed me she made direct eye contact. She looked down at me with a familiar glance of concern and then continued on her way.

I cried. I was completely destroyed. At that point she was my final lifeline, the light at the end of the tunnel. She was a window back into a world where I could be normal, or as close to it as I have ever been. But she had simply ignored me. Because I was a dirty-looking junky, she had carried on about her business.

People *were* objects. If this girl – the one person on earth who is everything to do with perfect – was willing to ignore me, to completely blank me, what hope was there? I thought about that all day. I had thought a lot about suicide. Before then I had even fantasised about something happening to me. Something tragic yet heroic that would end my life. I used to act out speeches at my funeral in my head. I would wonder how people would remember me. For some warped reason I found this comforting. The idea that I was dead was appealing to me. The process of killing myself was the only thing standing between me and my fantasy of death.

I knew I could take a ton of heroin and send myself into oblivion, but I didn't want to do that. That was too close to completely giving up. At least if I killed myself on my own, without drugs, it was, in a very small sense, a victory of sorts. I knew if I was wasted enough I could slit my wrists and feel little pain. But I always knew these thoughts were never going to be a reality. Although I had felt lows beyond description, I still knew I wasn't capable of actually killing myself. But Kelly ignoring me that day had brought me closer than I had ever been to the idea.

That day I walked for hours, which was hard to do. I had no muscles left. I wasn't really eating or drinking, so God knows why I didn't just die. I thought about Kelly, about all the fond memories I had of her and our relationship. How nice she was, not just to me, but also to everyone else. She was the most considerate person in the world and yet, because of the state I was in, she wouldn't even stop to talk to me. She hadn't seen me for years, why wasn't she at least curious, let alone concerned? Did I look that bad that she didn't even want to be seen in the same proximity as me?

I then realised that the situation was much worse than I had thought. I knew Kelly; I was right about her. She is the most warm-hearted person on the planet. She would stop and talk to me no matter what. She simply had not recognised me. I was that messed up. My face was a different shape, I had a beard, my hair was greasy, I was wearing dirty, baggy clothes and I was nearly half the weight I used to be. The idea that she would ignore me was impossible, but that she didn't recognise me? This was certainly feasible.

That realisation had two profound effects on me. First and foremost I was shocked that a person who I have been closer to than anyone else in the world didn't recognise me. But she hadn't ignored me. There was still hope, albeit a tiny amount.

That was it. That day I decided for sure that I was going to sort myself out. It was like a fork in the road, one route goes to a cliff that will certainly kill me and the other route holds a giant question mark. I chose the latter. With most addictions, deciding for sure that you are going to stop and actually stopping have very little to do with each other. Although that moment was the tipping point – I was now a junky trying to get off heroin, but I was still a junky.

I had a rotten time at the beginning. I tried a rehab procedure that lots of addicts go through which did help to a point. But I kept falling back into old routines. I was still acquainted with Sam, although I still firmly believed him to be no friend of mine. I took a cocktail of alternatives to heroin but most proved to be mere distractions. I rationalised that drinking and taking a wild combination of pills – painkillers and the like – was well worth the risk.

Even if I was very ill from the substances I used as a distraction, at least I wasn't ill from heroin or, worse, lack of heroin. I remember a really bad attempt at getting clean where I literally ran away. I thought it was quite an ingenious idea at the time. I had tried going cold turkey but it had made me way too ill. I really couldn't cope. I was genuinely worried the trauma of it would kill me and, if it didn't, the pain of it would certainly drive me to suicide. Although I had a glimmer of light at the end of the tunnel I still didn't care that much about my life. So one morning I ran to the train station and got on the first available train. I didn't get a ticket because I was aiming to get as far away as possible. If I could get myself to a town where I didn't know anyone, I could easily slip into a gutter somewhere and ride it out.

I ended up in a town that was dear to me; a town that I lived in when I was a toddler and moved from at about two years of age. The place still felt vaguely comforting. I assumed if I was going to be surviving without heroin it might as well be in a place slightly familiar to me. I consequently got arrested that evening, ironically nothing to do with heroin or my free train ride but rather I matched the description of a local robber. Obviously I wasn't the robber, which they later found out. The police, like so many others before, were concerned for me and were incredibly helpful even though I was a suspect and clearly a drug addict. Again, I found myself back home.

When coming off heroin there are lots of 'last times'. I lost count of how many last times I had had, but I will never forget the real one. I knew with confidence that it would be my last. I had decided that no matter how sick I became, no matter how painful it was that I would sooner die than put any more of it inside me. This was a turning point. The reason for relapsing so many times was of course because of how sick I became without it, but ultimately it came down to my fear of dying. I was confident I would die if I cut heroin out of my life completely. I wasn't scared any more, though. I said to myself that if it got too bad to handle I would just kill myself – rather than relapsing back into old habits. Although that sounds quite a chilling concept, it was actually quite comforting for me and proved a decision that, ironically, saved my live.

It has been almost a decade since I last touched heroin. These last years have been by far the toughest of my life. Soon after I was off it I had a terrible time. I was very depressed and simply could not make myself happy. I thought I had actually killed the part of my brain that made happiness possible. I had no aspirations, no hobbies and no friends.

I lived with my parents for a long time and held down a variety of steady jobs but found satisfaction, happiness or even a slightly positive attitude was something I simply could not achieve. Although I didn't touch heroin, my affection towards substances was far from over. I still drank way too much and smoked way too much. I even used to make a special kind of tea with a tremendous blend of painkillers in it. I thought about patenting the recipe at one point but realised that the quantities were borderline deadly.

Relatively, though, my drinking and painkiller abuse really wasn't too much of an issue. Even my parents didn't mind too much, either. So what if I drank in the morning? At least it wasn't heroin. I had clambered out of the fire but was taking a break in the frying pan; slow and steady wins the race.

This went on for a long time. I was so lonely. I used to sit for hours doing literally nothing. I would sit in my room with the TV on and stare at the wall behind it for hours. I wasn't even deep in thought, just in my zombie mode – quite an accurate name for it (thanks, dad).

It has been a fairly crazy journey to get to the point I am at now. I would have found it all so much easier if I had understood the power of time as a healer. This is applicable to all forms of pain. I wish I could have understood that things can get better, that time can change things in ways you can't imagine. Knowing what I know now would have made everything a lot easier.

I see kids on the street now, or hear stories in the news about addicts and wonder if I could help them. I then imagine if, at my worst state, an ex-addict had tried to get through to me, and I realise that you can't save people from themselves. A person needs to change inside before outside influences become anything more than just noise. For me there were poignant moments that all added up to a change. This needs to be understood for other addicts. You can sit them down and talk things through. You can add slithers of doubt to their lifestyle. You can even scare them, shock them or disgust them into thinking twice but until they look at themselves in the mirror and make those crucial decisions you might as well be talking to a brick wall. Helping people get to that stage is a great thing to pursue, but expecting to have an effect on them before they get there themselves is just naive.

I spoke to Kelly a few years after the incident on the street and I was right. She didn't recognise me. We stayed in contact for a while – even after she had moved to Australia. We even promised each other, just like with university, that we would write and visit once in a while. We have since drifted apart once again and I haven't heard a peep from her for almost two years. It is not a problem, though. Our relationship has nothing to do with time. She is special to me no matter what happens and I think I am the same to her. Every time we speak there is a closeness that is irrespective of how long it has been since we last spoke.

Sam and I drifted out of contact completely. I live about five minutes away from one of his many dodgy cousins so I am surprised our paths have not crossed since. Last I heard he was still involved with heroin and still up to his old tricks. I don't hold anything against him but I have absolutely no desire to see him. I suppose far into the future, if one day he does get clean, we could have a relationship because there is still a lot I like about him. I still remember things we did together and burst out laughing, sometimes in rather inappropriate places. Yes, I am the strange spontaneous laugher you sometimes see in the supermarket!

Now I live alone and I have been working in the same job for more than two years. I work in a very strange office with an eccentric bunch of individuals and it feels like a family. I have a girlfriend, of almost three years, who is out of my league in every way. She is wonderful. She teaches dance classes, so I have picked a few moves up along the way. Turns out I truly understand three things (maths, painting and now salsa!). I even think I am happy now.

I have told her a bit about my past but have never told her quite how bad it was and I don't think I ever will. My past is exactly that, it is 'my past'. I am fully deserting it and moving on completely. That person, that version of me, is dead.

We had a conversation about children a few weeks ago and it turns out we both want to have some, but not for a little while. I wonder how much I would tell my children about my past. I think if they probe I will be honest, but as far as I am concerned I want my past to be buried.

If I am going to continue believing that I am entirely a new person, the memories of my past have no relevance in my life now. I am lucky enough to have been as low as I think it is possible to go – this means I now have very little to fear. I only hope that time carries on working its magic and continues to heal. I would also love to dig deep inside myself, analyse my life, and see if I can find something positive that has come from my addiction. I keep looking but am yet to find anything.

# ANN DOWN...

## ... ON ALMOST DROWNING WHILE WHITE-WATER RAFTING

> *'I was smashed repeatedly against the same rock; it felt like I was being punched over and over again. I did not have the strength to keep my face above the tormenting water; I frantically scrambled with all my might but couldn't get free. I coughed as I gasped for air, and panic set in. I was drowning.'*

I am not the strongest swimmer in the world so perhaps white-water rafting isn't the best sport for me. Nevertheless a few years back, my then boyfriend and I were on holiday in the States where he had the bright idea of doing a spot of white-water rafting to which I agreed – after a certain amount of persuasion.

He was a bit of an adrenaline junky. During our relationship he even dragged me on a tandem skydive. He had been rafting in that very spot before, on Gauley River, but the whole sport was relatively new to me.

We had been on tamer rapids the year before – the experts won't let you just jump into the most dangerous rivers because you can die if you don't have the experience. So, to a certain extent, I knew what I was doing but I was still 'out of my depth' – for want of a better phrase. I was in all the safety gear: life jacket, helmet etc. I knew that what we were doing was dangerous so cutting corners wasn't ever going to be my downfall.

Anyway, on our first afternoon we were on one of the stretches of river that is said to be particularly dangerous; it is Class 5 (with 6 being the highest) so it was very dodgy. I was a little nervous as I had never before been on any rapids quite this violent. But everyone I was with was relatively experienced, so I stayed calm and composed.

We were perhaps halfway down when things got really hairy. The boat had turned twice where it shouldn't have and the tone of everyone's orders got very serious. The atmosphere wasn't one of fun any more but rather genuine danger, which is fun for some I suppose. The raft twisted and jammed itself on a rock. I was being thrown around like a rag doll on the back of this thing, but I was doing all I was told, when I was told, and we pushed on.

There was a drop with raging rapids coming in from two different sources, we barrelled down and exactly the same thing happened once again. The raft twisted and turned, but this time I couldn't hold on. I really felt like a fragile toy, I was completely at the mercy of the water. I was catapulted out of the raft with an astonishing amount of force. It felt like it was happening in slow motion and, although I can't have gone that far into the air, it felt like I was thrown very high indeed. Everyone, apart from two people, had been flung out of the raft at that point but of course I didn't realise this at the time. I couldn't take in what was happening as it was all over in a flash.

After a split second of what seemed like silence in mid air (it was almost peaceful), I smashed backwards into the worst part of the noisy rapids below, plunging into the furious whirlpool. I was shunted straight into a rock, and then into another. I was very badly winded – I could not breathe. However, my head was above the water because of my life jacket, which was doing its job very well. I know if I had not been wearing it I would have been in a lot more trouble.

Within moments I was whipped and then pinned down in a very awkward crevice between two rocks with the relentless water bashing into me. I was smashed repeatedly against the same rock; it felt like I was being punched over and over again. I did not have the strength to keep my face above the tormenting water; I frantically scrambled with all my might but couldn't get free. I coughed as I gasped for air, and panic set in. I was drowning.

It was just non-stop; it wouldn't give me a break. I think if I had had more strength I could have kept my mouth and nose above the water but, after being so dazed from the impact and beginning to panic, I didn't stand a chance. I would get a flash of light, and then my face would be barraged once again. I couldn't say how long I was stuck there, it might have been just a few seconds but it seemed like a lifetime. I couldn't figure out why I was so stuck, maybe my jacket got snagged, or maybe it was just an unlucky combination of my weakness and my position, either way the result was that I *was* stuck. The water was stronger than me; I was fighting a losing battle.

It was hugely surreal as the next thing I saw was my boyfriend biting his fingernails, but on land. It was just like I had blinked, wished I was safe and – hey presto – it had worked! But in actual fact I had lost consciousness, which I assume happened against that rock but I cannot be sure.

Apparently my unconscious body had drifted downstream, over some more rocks to another bottleneck. I was dragged out as quickly as they could get to me but they assumed I was dead. One of the men resuscitated me and I have no doubt that he saved my life. He was a stranger to me and yet he did everything he could to help me and eventually brought me back from certain death.

I was very sick when I woke up. A nightmarish amount of water came out of me and even though it wasn't the most dignifying display (as it was coming out of my nose) I was so happy to be out of the water and I wanted the water out of me.

I had no serious injuries but I had bruising all over my body. I tried but couldn't find a part of me that didn't ache for days afterwards. The worst, strangely enough, was on my bum cheek. It felt like I had been hit on the bottom with a hammer – I couldn't sit down for a long time!

No one saw what had happened to me so they assumed I had fallen unconscious immediately, but I explained that I remembered it all (until I passed out that is); falling out of the raft as well as being bashed against the rocks. My boyfriend said that he thought I was dead as I hadn't moved for so long, and then he went on to say that he was more worried about explaining my death to my parents than anything else, which was sweet of him.

Even after a near-death experience I have actually been rafting since, even on that same river. I have also become a much stronger swimmer but I will still do my best not to jump into any rapids any time soon.

# DAVID STONE...

## ... ON THE BLOOD POISONING THAT NEARLY KILLED HIM

*'I guess it was worth all the pain because now they knew exactly what was wrong with me. I had several large liver abscesses. Apparently the bacteria had somehow entered my bloodstream and settled in my liver, which was fighting a losing battle to survive against it. I was dying.'*

I was twenty-three and my first child had just been born a week earlier when I began to feel ill. I had all the classic symptoms of flu. For a few days it just kept getting worse and worse. By the third day I was no longer able to eat or drink anything and would bring back even a teaspoon of water if I swallowed it.

I began to wonder if there was something seriously wrong with me, but my wife kept telling me, rather harshly, to 'shut up, stop moaning and take it like a man!' She was convinced it was just flu and I was being over the top!

By the sixth day I decided, after three days with no food or water, that I was going to see a doctor... except it was a Sunday.

Instead I phoned the NHS advice line and they suggested that I visit the hospital. My wife protested, 'They'll just send you home and you'll look like an idiot!'

The doctor called me in and after the usual formalities he took my temperature. He said it was rather odd that I was sweating so profusely, because I was cold to the touch. He then suggested that it was OK for me to remain in hospital because things were relatively quiet and they would probably have a bed available for me quite soon.

I remember thinking, 'Now look who's overreacting!' but I turned and saw my wife's face and suddenly she looked different, like she now realised this could be something serious.

They put me in a little side room on a main ward, unsure if I might need to be quarantined. My family started showing up and were all wondering why I wasn't lying on the bed. 'It's OK,' I reassured them, 'it's not like I'm staying is it!'

A few minutes later someone pointed out my shoe was untied, so I bent over to tie it, and passed out. From that moment on, everything was very different. Suddenly the medical staff who had been largely ignoring me were all fussing like crazy, shining lights in my eyes and lying me down with the bed angled so that all the blood rushed to my head. I looked at my family, the people who had been laughing and joking around me like we were at the pub. Their faces now had the same expression as my wife – the 'I don't know what to say' face.

Things went blurry after that. I had passed out because I had blood poisoning, but they still didn't know why. They did tests on my blood and found Streptococcus, bacteria usually found in the mouth, where it generally stays. They still didn't know why it was in my blood or what the main cause of the problem was. They wanted to know if I had been to India or eaten in any unusual places. I hadn't.

On the second day they decided I was getting worse and put me in intensive care. I was treated very nicely in there and looking back I wonder if it was because they all thought I was going to die. It turns out that's what my family had all concluded. They gave me morphine... the doctors that is, not my family. I had a little push-button that would release more on intervals but not too much.

That's when things got really blurry. I remember a doctor coming in to tell me that he needed to make an incision in my neck so that he could insert a tube into my heart – not exactly something you forget no matter how much morphine you've had! It hurt – it hurt like hell. The tube was large enough that it had six more tubes inside, each of which was wider than a standard needle. I could feel it scraping down my neck, just under my skin.

After that there was a period of blankness. In my mind, to this day, I am quite convinced I spent only three days in intensive care. But apparently I was there for a whole week.

On the third day they took me for an MRI scan. They made me lie on a stiff board and hold my breath. I was in more pain than I had ever been in, in my life; I even told them that it was more tempting not to breathe than to endure the pain of breathing. It felt like I was in that machine forever. It was loud, claustrophobic and I was quite literally suffocating myself. Finally they let me out and put me back on a soft bed where I could breathe more easily.

I guess it was worth all the pain because now they knew exactly what was wrong with me. I had several large liver abscesses. Apparently the bacteria had somehow entered my bloodstream and settled in my liver, which was fighting a losing battle to survive against it. I was dying.

To treat me I had, at one stage, three tubes going into me and was wearing an oxygen mask constantly. One drip was fluids, one was antibiotics, and one was, of course, morphine. They assigned a specialist to me, who told my family she had only ever seen one case like this, a month ago, and that man had died. Joy!

But luck was on my side, because by the end of my second week in hospital I had started to recover. I was moved to a main ward and was now on a single drip. They brought in a physiotherapist to help me walk again, as your muscles are seriously affected by not eating or moving for two and a half weeks. I still had to have a nurse to take me to the toilet.

I then looked at myself in the mirror for the first time, and was utterly horrified by what I saw. I had lost two and a half stone, thirty-five pounds, in just two and a half weeks. I looked like a severe anorexic and my skin and eyes were yellow.

But I was getting better. I started to eat, although nothing tasted the same. I tried coffee with no sugar but it was still too sweet.

At the end of the third week I was in a lot of pain again, and it turned out the infection had spread to my right lung, directly over the liver – I had caught pneumonia.

They decided they needed to test the fluid build-up in my lung to see if it was infected or was just fluid that would be reabsorbed eventually. To do so, they told me they needed to insert a needle into my lung through my back... for which they brought in a student doctor!

Back in the MRI scanner I had been certain I'd felt the worst pain there was to feel. That student proved me wrong. He missed the gap between the ribs, somehow, and scraped the sharp point of the needle against my bone. It hurt so much that I instantly vomited, and the experienced doctor responded by suggesting he withdraw and start again! The next time he did exactly the same thing! And the result, after the doctor had taken over, was that the fluid wasn't even infected.

Almost a month after I went into hospital, where I had missed four of my son's first six weeks of life, I was finally released, after begging and begging them to let me go just for the sake of my mental health, regardless of my physical state.

It was a mistake. My own bed was so painful that in order to lie down I had to lie on my side for a whole minute holding my breath waiting for the pain to subside, and then finally I could roll onto my back where I was able to just about breathe enough to stay alive. Two days later the fluid in my lung now *was* infected, and I was back in hospital.

Fortunately it didn't last long and I've now fully recovered. I have regained the missing pounds and then some!

Leaving the hospital, seeing the building shrink away into the distance, was one of the greatest feelings I have ever had. That night I stood beside my own bed, fell to my knees and cried for what seemed like hours. I was finally free.

Eventually the hospital agreed on what had caused it all. I'd had a dental abscess and refused to visit the dentist and eventually it went away, but only because it went to my liver. The moral of this story is therefore quite obvious: don't fear the dentist, because far worse things could happen without them!

# KAYT WEBSTER-BROWN...

## ... ON BEING HIT BY A CAR

---

*'The windscreen smashed as it made contact with my forehead, knocking me unconscious. My body was limp and flailing. I flew ten feet in the air before meeting the concrete by the side of the road.'*

---

We walked up the hill clutching Sainsbury's bags full of bottles and cans. We were laughing and joking; ready for a night out on 'the green'. This was a standard Friday night for us fourteen-year-olds. It was nothing too exciting, but there was a fairly large crowd of like-minded youngsters looking to have a good time.

We got to the edge of the road, ready to cross over to the green – our town's famous spot for under-age drinking. A few passed over, others waited for oncoming traffic to pass. I stood, looking left, looking right. I looked left again and saw headlights in the distance; I tried to judge how far away they were and whether or not I still had time to cross.

Again, I looked. I had enough time. 'You can go now,' I thought. A final look... I can definitely still make it...

The windscreen smashed as it made contact with my forehead, knocking me unconscious. My body was limp and flailing. I flew ten feet in the air before meeting the concrete by the side of the road. If I hadn't passed out, the injuries may have been much more severe. As it stood, I was left with a broken arm, the other fractured, a broken ankle and damage to my pelvis.

Flashing lights, blackness, voices, skin, an unusual perspective, figures towering over me, more blackness, flashing lights and then reality. I knew what the ache was before I'd even realised what had happened; you just know these things when they happen to you. Even if your consciousness has been elsewhere, your brain still had to stick around for the ride. It knows.

It all seemed to happen in a different order than it possibly could have done. The first memory I have is of opening my eyes and feeling some kind of strange déjà vu. I remember seeing flashing blue lights down the road ahead of me from my twisted viewpoint on the floor. I asked if it was a dream. It sure felt like one.

I remember slipping in and out of awareness. It's like you see in films – flashes from a viewpoint, then moving figures and murmured voices. The gaps are filled in with darkness and no real perception of time can be grasped. There seemed to be some kind of progress, though. Something was happening but people were still pacing, looking panicked. Most were standing with one arm folded and the other resting on it; hand on mouth, legs apart. People lean down to the camera, and everyone wants to hold your hand. Then it hits a scene and there's movement. Jilted camera angles and muffled voices that sound too close to the speakers.

Then you realise that you're the main character and that whatever happened, happened to you. Then there's no more blackness. No void to escape to, and time is still all messed up but this time it's real. It's now and it isn't a dream, but it still feels like one. Except, unlike a dream, there's pain and it's real. It's a dumb pain, but it's definitely real.

Then they tried rolling me onto a giant chopping board; this long, hard, flat plastic thing. Suddenly I appreciated the comfort of the concrete like never before. There was comfort in stillness and in unconsciousness.

'What day is it?' they asked.

'I don't fucking know... Monday?' I took a stab in the dark.

What kind of question is that? Then they asked for a number. That's an easy one. I recited my dad's mobile number without a second thought.

The woman standing over me under the bright lights of the ambulance's interior had short-cropped hair. There were a few people over me, shining torches into my eyes, asking stupid questions that I didn't really care to answer. I hated them from the start. I hated all of them. This was simply a hassle; trouble in my life I didn't need. They were linked to this hassle and they were strangers I had no care for.

It seemed like seconds had passed before I was being wheeled out over concrete in the night with my friend running alongside. My parents had been at a concert in London; they were called out from the concert hall and came as soon as they'd heard what had happened. Other than my ankle of which they had already been informed was broken, my parents had no clue what the damage was.

My face was covered in blood from where my head hit the windscreen. When my parents arrived, my friend – still in shock – told them to leave. She said that I was OK and that she could take care of me. Of course, they didn't leave.

I only remember my mum being with me. I suppose my dad was waiting somewhere else. I was taken to a room where they relocated my broken ankle. I think that is the single most painful experience I've ever had in my life, and I certainly didn't keep it to myself.

I can't remember at what point it was they cut my clothes off, but I hated it. It was cold that night so I'd worn layers, lots of layers. I was wearing all my favourite clothes and they just ripped them apart like they were paper.

I have never sworn so much in my entire life as I did that night. You name it – I said it. Every curse word I knew spilled out from my mouth, echoing through the hospital wards. I expect the extent of my x-rated diction probably took my mother aback a little. I didn't care; it hurt and I wanted everyone to know just how much.

There was one guy I liked at the hospital, although I can't remember his name. I remember there were two guys with the same name. I think they were both all right, but one made jokes and was nice to me despite the abuse I had no doubt given him, so I warmed to him a bit.

It all seemed almost insignificant at the time. Just like most of the people working there at the hospital. There were lots of people I didn't like. I didn't like the woman that tried to move me by my broken arm when she was slipping a bedpan under me, for example. It was humiliating enough as it was but she was stupid, awkward and wouldn't look me in the eye. Although when she did, it was just to patronise me. I remember I didn't like the abrupt Scottish woman who tried to get me to do Christmas arts and crafts.

I'd tell you it wasn't all doom and gloom but it really, really was! It was truly awful. My week in hospital was the worst week of my life and the duration for which I couldn't walk was just an extended version of that week but without the crap food and annoying people.

In hospital I missed people. When I left, I missed walking. I never knew how much I loved it until that point. I used to walk everywhere. Being fourteen, I relied on my parents for transport but I still loved to walk. I loved the freedom of it and I especially loved walking in the rain.

I lay in bed for days, imagining what I'd do when I was free to walk again. I wanted a long leather coat. I wanted to walk to the edge of town and everywhere through it, wearing this coat and a pair of boots. I told my parents I wanted one and they found it for me. It was perfect and only £20 in a charity shop. I really loved that coat. Even though I never actually went on that walk, it always meant something. It was like a souvenir or a mascot for freedom, for love and appreciation for the simple things in life.

I wrote a lot. I thought a lot. I watched daytime TV a lot. I developed a strange excitement for *Ally McBeal*. My friends visited me and I bought their Christmas presents online. I remember one day it snowed and they came to see me after school. I saw them playing in the snow outside my house and I felt envy like never before.

I still loved them but I saw their individual friendships strengthening and felt ours growing weaker. I wasn't there every day to keep the connection strong; not there to laugh with them, trip them up, go out and play in fields or get drunk with them. I was not able to see them outside the walls of my parents' house. I was off school for just over two months but overall I made a relatively fast recovery.

I remember one day my dad took me out food shopping for Christmas. I had to go in a wheelchair. Despite my disability being temporary, I have never felt more beneath people in my life. He amused himself by wheeling me into things but I hated the lack of control. But more than anything I hated the lack of eye contact. I never want to be in a wheelchair again.

Seven years on and I still have the bolts they put in my ankle to hold the bone together. They had to re-operate because, after I left the hospital the first time, I was under the instruction that I should walk on my broken ankle to strengthen it. I think that was the worst advice I have ever been given!

When I found out the bones had moved and they had to re-operate, I couldn't stop crying. I was told that if they didn't, I was likely to have such bad arthritis by the time I was nineteen that I'd be unable to walk at all.

I didn't care at the time. I said I'd rather do that than go through it all again. The thought of starting over practically killed me and any option that meant that didn't have to happen seemed far more appealing to me at that moment in time. But I had the operation and, again, made a speedy recovery.

My ankle still gets achy and stiff in the cold, or if I crouch on it for too long. I have a scar to show for it, along with two on my arm where it had two petal pins sticking out to hold the bone together.

A lot changed over that time. It was intense and I grew up a lot emotionally. I'd never take it back as I truly believe everything happens for a reason but it's definitely not something I intend to seek out again anytime soon.

# MARTIN JONES...

## ... ON LOSING HIS SIGHT AND THEN REGAINING IT TWELVE YEARS LATER

*'When the bandages came off it was like looking through water in a swimming pool, at first I could just see light. Then steadily it was as though the water drained away, and I could see. It was incredible. I had been blind for twelve years and now I had my vision back — it was amazing.'*

Back in 1996 I was working as a self-employed plasterer. It was early in February, which is a time of year when work tended to drop off a bit. A friend of mine arranged for me to come and do some casual work at a scrap yard for a while, just to tide me over.

Even though I hadn't been trained to do so, we were melting aluminium; wheels and engine parts etc. I had been working there around three weeks. It was 3 February and there was snow on the ground. I had got the first melt all ready and gone for my morning break; after my break I knew it would be hot enough to pour out into the ingot mould.

I went into the shed where the furnace was and, leaning over the mould, I started pouring the molten aluminium. For a split second I noticed a hissing. I don't know if it happens to other people, but I have had it happen twice in my life now. I had a serious bicycle accident in my teens. During the accident everything went into slow motion.

That hissing probably lasted mere milliseconds but still I had time to think, 'Where's that coming from?' all in slow motion. 'It must be water that's in the cast iron moulds – this is going to explode.'

I have since been told by health and safety executives that, although there was no visible water in the moulds, because cast iron is porous the water had soaked into the metal. So when the molten aluminium was poured on, it created super steam which expanded to sixteen times its size. As this steam was surrounded by molten aluminium, it had nowhere to go.

It exploded. I suffered thirty-seven per cent burns, as the explosion was 600°C. When it exploded, I was standing directly over it but the damage was done mostly to my left-hand side. But because I was so close it also got my right eye. They still have the pieces of metal in my file at the hospital. They are a bit smaller than a five pence piece and a tiny bit thinner than a pound coin, so it was quite a chunk of metal that ended up lodged in my eye.

I thought straight away I should get some water on the damage. I thought I should put my face in the snow, then I remembered that the ground was covered in car parts and oil; not what you want to rub into a wound. I decided against that option.

The explosion had been heard in the office, so all the staff, including my friend (who arranged the work), came to see what had happened.

'Is it bad?' I asked him.

'No no, you'll be all right.'

I asked him again and he confessed, 'Yeah, it's really bad.'

I couldn't see. My eye lids had been burnt together.

I was taken to my local hospital, Rotherham, but my injuries were too serious for them. The nearest specialised burns unit was the Northern General in Sheffield. They were in two minds; they didn't know whether to deal with the burns first or deal with the eyesight first.

They decided to start with the burns. Burns cause more pain when they are exposed to air. So they put cream on and wrapped me up in cling film, which basically stops the air getting to the wound and relieves some of the pain.

I knew for a fact that I was blind at that point; you just know these things. A couple of weeks before I had twisted my ankle; the irony being had I actually broken it I would have been off work that day. Strangely I was concerned about my ankle and kept asking the nurses to be careful with it. It was really hurting. I had metal lodged in my eyes, virtually no skin on the top half of my body and yet I was more worried about my ankle. I think my body couldn't cope with the amount of pain that I was in, so what it did was concentrate on the pain it could deal with. At the time I could hardly feel my burns, but I was very aware of my ankle.

It was later confirmed that I had lost sight in both eyes. I was also told that the left one had to be removed straight away because it was so damaged. Infection would have been too big a risk to leave it in.

My left eyelid was glued together with the hope that in fifteen years' time or so eye transplant technology could be available. We're still a little bit off full eye transplants but one day, hopefully, that procedure will be possible. My right eye, although badly damaged, was left in place. I was told it could be removed and replaced with a glass eye but at that time technology was improving and significant developments were being made towards procedures that could cure blindness. So the eye was left in to give me a better chance in the future. It was certainly worthwhile keeping my right eye in place.

I stayed in hospital for around four months to have treatment for my injuries. I accepted it all straight away; I didn't have any regrets. I thought, 'OK, something bad has happened, but I'm not dead.' I was still alive so there were still things that I could do. The nurses commented to my visitors just how accepting I was of being blind.

I was told back then, when seeing my consultant, that a new pioneering procedure was becoming available. He explained that a tooth could be taken out of my mouth and placed in my eye with a lens built in which might allow me to see. At that time, around twelve years ago, he had only done it a couple of times and they were not that confident about the process. I was told that it could only be done once and if it didn't work, that would be it – I would be blind forever.

There was another option which was a stem cell operation and that could be repeated if it failed. It was my decision, either the surgery that might regain my sight, but can only be tried once, or the stem cell option that could be repeated. It scared me a little bit that the operation could only be done once; it kept a few doubts in my mind. Those doubts prevented me from going through with the procedure at that point.

I learned to function without my sight. I learned how to use a cane. I got involved with a local charity where I was approached to do some training for people who care for visually impaired individuals. It was a great opportunity, so I accepted.

Care home staff used the training quite a lot because the majority of blind people are over sixty-five. Consequently my future wife, Gill, who worked for a care home had come on the training.

I was outside on one of the training days, just having a cigarette, and she approached me and asked if she was in the right place for the training. I told her she was, gave her directions and in she went. She didn't realise until I went back inside that I was actually the trainer!

We had a good laugh together and she came back twice more. On the third training day we got together and we eventually ended up getting married. Obviously I had never seen her at this point.

We went on a fantastic five-week honeymoon. I wanted a good one as I was only getting married once; she arranged the wedding so it was left up to me to organise the honeymoon.

I thought I would take her on a cruise, which landed us in Bermuda for ten days.

I kept all our destinations, which included New York, Los Angeles and Las Vegas, a secret until the day before we arrived in each. The trip came to an end when we arrived in Australia to spend a week visiting her brothers who live out there.

Everyday I gave her a piece of paper with the location on. When she found out we were visiting her brothers she was ecstatic.

Shortly after we returned, we moved house. In the midst of our move we received a call informing me that a stem cell donor had become available. The operation had to be carried out within forty-eight hours, though. So we had to arrange to get from Rotherham to Nottingham the next day.

During the operation everything was going fine but all of a sudden the stem cells just disappeared. I was told that it hadn't worked. However, from there I was passed onto a consultant, Christopher Liu, at the Sussex Eye Clinic in Brighton, who had been getting more and more success with the procedure whereby a tooth would be placed in my eye, which could allow me to see.

We went to see him and it turned out that my eye was in good condition for him to work on. In fact, it was almost ideal. It essentially hadn't been touched because it had been under a layer of skin, which had been taken out of my mouth to protect the eye. It was actually acting as a conjunctiva which I had lost in the accident. It hadn't been touched so the eye was exactly as it was twelve years ago. This was great news for me as it meant he could operate with this pioneering procedure.

I was told that there was around a seventy-five per cent chance that I would get some sight back. Even the consultant didn't know exactly how much sight I would get back, if any, but we thought it was worth a try.

It is an amazing procedure. They took a canine tooth out of my mouth, reshaped it, drilled a hole in it and put a lens in. Then it was placed inside my cheek for about three months. Over that time the tooth begins to get its own blood supply and it starts growing fibrous tissue. As soon as that happens the tooth can be pulled out of the cheek and it'll cling to the eye.

I told Gill that I wanted her to be with me. I wanted her to be the first person I saw when the bandages came off. I told Mr Liu, who was very considerate and said that, although he had to remove the dressing, he could accommodate my wishes and let me see Gill first, if I could see at all.

I was excited; I was fine about the bandages coming off and was eager to see the results of the operation. Gill, on the other hand, was a nervous wreck in the hotel. I had never seen her so she was really worried about what I would think when I did. She worried I might not like her.

When the bandages came off it was like looking through water in a swimming pool, at first I could just see light. Then steadily it was as though the water drained away, and I could see. It was incredible. I had been blind for twelve years and now I had my vision back – it was amazing.

My vision did come and go for quite a few months because there was skin growing over the lens. So sometimes I could see for two weeks or so and then I would go blind again. But, in March 2008, that issue was rectified and I have been able to see ever since. I can see well now, all I need glasses for is reading. My eyesight might have declined to that point anyway because of my age, irrespective of my accident. So it really is great what has been done.

Now I appreciate everything a lot more. I used to appreciate the world, but in a very different way. Regaining my sight has meant that now Gill and I can do things that before we couldn't. Simple things like sitting down and watching a film together is now possible.

I have been able to see for more than a year but I am still looking around and appreciating all the colours and beauty in the world. As I used to work as a plasterer, construction has always interested me. So now I can look at buildings once again.

Obviously things are more relaxed for Gill now, for example we recently went on holiday to Egypt and where as she used to have to do all the navigating now I can do some too. I no longer need to be guided around as well. Although she never, ever complained about doing things to help me, now I can do them all myself.

I've always loved exploring, finding new things, and now I can see, it all means so much more. When you've had something, then you've lost it, then you regain it you appreciate it a lot more.

I started a job when my eyesight became stable. Going back into employment has been great; it gives me a sense of achievement that I think was missing when I was blind. Something else that has changed is when I was blind everything used to talk to me. I had a speaking watch, microwave, computer etc. I don't miss their monotonous voices. Also now talking books are a thing of the past – I can read them myself.

For lots of blind people, feeling somebody's face helps them gain a mental picture of what they might look like. But for me, maybe because I had sight and then lost it, that was never the case, so I didn't really have a mental image of what my wife might look like.

When my bandages came off and I saw her for the first time, though, it was fantastic. I fell in love with her all over again.

# ERIC COLON...

## ... ON SURVIVING A WILD DOG'S VICIOUS ATTACK

---

'The pain was incredible. It was like a vice grip squeezing the flesh on my forearm. I could feel each one of its teeth grinding the bone and tendons. I could see the amount of damage it was doing as it whipped its head backwards and forwards. It was as if he was trying to peel my arm like a banana.'

---

I have always loved animals, especially dogs, but on one of my recent Spanish holidays I encountered first-hand how dangerous they can be.

I was enjoying a short break with my partner and nine-year-old son in Spain; we were staying at a lovely hotel and the holiday was going great. The morning before we left to head home to the UK I went for one last walk with my boy to say farewell to the place.

We walked from the hotel towards the beach, choosing to take an alternative route than we had taken before. It was about 10 a.m. and, although the road we were walking on had been busy days earlier, today it was very quiet and there wasn't a soul in sight. Anyway, we were near the beach when we walked alongside what used to be a courtyard for a cafe, which was now completely derelict. I saw a couple of stray dogs not far from where we were.

I had noticed one of the dogs a few days before when it had been loitering around near the hotel, but I hadn't paid much attention to it as there were lots of stray dogs in the area. Now, though, it caught my eye. I am unsure of the breed, but it was wolf-like and seemed quite well-fed unlike a lot of local strays. I saw that the animal had blood on its head. I positioned my son on the other side of me as we continued on our way. This dog was visibly unhappy with us being nearby. It began to grumble a vicious 'go away' growl. We obliged.

We took a different route back to the hotel as I didn't want to encounter the dog again. I wasn't scared as such because I have always felt a connection and understanding with dogs but I was suitably wary of this particular one. I was completely right to be wary.

We headed back. We were perhaps 100 m from the back entrance to the hotel's pool area when the dog appeared yet again, pretty much from nowhere, in front of us. It began growling and barking as it once again wanted us to leave. I was happy to stay out of this dog's way but the track was narrow so it meant we had to head back on ourselves. I told my son not to worry as we started to retrace our steps. The dog stayed close though. I didn't want to antagonise it further by speeding up, plus I knew that picking my son up and running would scare him a great deal.

The dog was getting closer and closer though; it was behaving very strangely. Usually if a dog growls in a territorial way, simply leaving calms the situation, but not today. It happened in a flash – I can't actually remember the dog jumping or me doing anything erratic to encourage the attack.

Before I knew what was happening the dog had jumped up and sunk its teeth into me. It grazed my forearm as I fell to the ground. Within moments I had noticed blood, but I wasn't at all worried about myself, only that the dog might turn on my son. I screamed, in a very aggressive way, at my son to go and get help. I wanted to make it absolutely clear that he had to go away. I was worried that he might try and get the dog off me, which could easily get him hurt. I yelled at him to run and get help, which thankfully he did. He sprinted towards the hotel whilst I held the dog in place above me.

The dog was ferocious. It was behaving like a police dog that you see on TV. It was pulling and tugging and ripping my shirt. It began mauling me as I fended off its bites. Luckily for me it seemed too frantic and angry to get a hold of my neck, although I could see that is what he was aiming for. Lying on my back I mustered enough strength to shove the dog off me to my side.

I scrambled to a kneeling position but again the crazed animal went for me. I put my arm up and it sunk its first proper bite in and I was back on the floor with the dog over me once again. The pain was incredible. It was like a vice grip squeezing the flesh on my forearm. I could feel each one of its teeth grinding the bone and tendons. I could see the amount of damage it was doing as it whipped its head backwards and forwards. It was as if he was trying to peel my arm like a banana.

There were a few calm moments where the dog seemed to take a break but he would never stop growling and sniffing. It would sit still, but remain clamped down on my arm. I would try and shove it off but this would just exacerbate things. I started genuinely worrying at this point. Up until then I never thought the dog would be strong enough to actually kill me but I was getting so weak. I had lost a huge amount of blood and thought that if I blacked out he would be able to bite me wherever he pleased, which would not be good. It really was like a nightmare. I was completely at the dog's mercy. I had lost all my strength by this point. Even when I pushed as hard as I possibly could I was aware that I wasn't even one tenth as strong as the dog was.

The attack must have taken around three minutes but it felt like hours. I was covered in blood and my arm looked like it had been in a blender; skin was dangling in threads. I had given up fighting by the time help arrived, I was simply waiting.

Help did arrive though, in the form of the hotel manager. He came storming down the track towards us with two staff members behind him. He approached the situation and with the most incredibly casual strength he grabbed the dog and pulled it away. I didn't see exactly what he did but by the time I had realised the dog was not on me any more I saw it lying, completely still, by my side. He had killed it, somehow. I remember his words exactly as, had I not been in so much shock, I would have been laughing. With a spectacularly blasé tone he sighed, shook his head and mumbled in his thick Spanish accent, 'silly dog'.

He removed his shirt and wrapped it tight around my arm and then helped me to my feet. He then took me in his car to the local hospital where my arm was sorted out. I also had a bad cut on my head from falling over that I hadn't even noticed until I got to the emergency room.

I had surgery in the UK where the flesh on my forearm had been kind of 'rebuilt'. Now I have weird lumpy scars but other than that you'd never know. I am extremely grateful to the heroic hotel man as if he hadn't turned up when he did, I am confident I would have been very badly hurt – maybe even died. I am also so grateful that my son wasn't hurt. He didn't even seem that bothered by the whole event – we were even making jokes about it later that day.

I almost felt slightly sorry for the dog; it obviously had something wrong with it. I don't know whether the blood it had on it was from an injury it sustained, which may have caused it to go mental, or whether it was simply blood from another tourist it tried to eat earlier that day. Either way, I couldn't muster up too much sympathy for it as he was a very bad dog indeed.

# SIOBHAN PEAL...

## ... ON BECOMING A WOMAN AFTER LIVING AS A MAN FOR MORE THAN FIFTY YEARS

*'I was locked rigid and I felt a massive surge of unknown energy start in my lower body, run through my torso to the nape of my neck and release straight into my brain. I tried to stop it and couldn't, realising that whatever it was, was somehow correct. This repeated eight times taking about two hours and that was it, I was all female, all switched on correctly and the male side was switched off. It was fantastic; the most wonderful feeling in the world.'*

Perhaps the best place to begin is to clear up the use and meaning of particular words. Whilst I am described by the outside world as 'transsexual', I prefer 'transgender'. Transsexual as a word seems to muddle people up as it holds connotations about sexuality. In actual fact sexual orientation has nothing to do with gender. It is an entirely separate area of the brain. A lot of people mix up transgender with transvestite, which is unfortunate. Transvestite relates to wearing clothes from the opposite gender and also holds connotations of sexuality. A transgendered individual may well do this but their reasons are entirely different. Unfortunately the symptoms can appear very similar and individuals often go through an experimental phase whilst trying to find themselves.

There are two kinds of transgendered people. Primary is someone who discovers it all when they are young, generally in the teenage years and often these are the ones that really suffer. I am the secondary kind, as I discovered that I was female relatively late in life. Children up to the age of about seven wouldn't know either way, but when you get to that age onwards, gender in the mind starts to kick in. For those who are like myself, male to female (female to male is around a quarter of the ratio and I can't speak for them) it is as though you literally form a facade around yourself but you don't know you're doing it.

The best way to describe it is to think of acting. Successful actors are fantastic because they become the part that they play on stage. When you are transgendered you become the apparent physical gender – in my case – male, but it is an acting facade and it is so powerful that you don't even realise you're in a play. You look as though you're male, the testosterone in you operates in the way it should but it is a falsehood as it is overriding the core of the brain, which is in fact female. How this appears to the outside world is unique to each of us. I cannot speak for others but only illustrate from my own experience.

Originally I didn't ever think about transgendered people. Why would I need to? It was completely irrelevant to me. When I was a teenager, as a boy, I was male to all intents and purposes. One difference I noticed, though, was that I didn't react to girls in the same way as other boys my age. There was no sexual drive towards females so on a scale of one to ten, in terms of a 'normal' male sex drive I would guess I was around one. In hindsight I've really got nobody to compare myself with, as I don't know what the normal amount of sex drive is. A real boy would know but I was never a real boy; it was an act and it was being driven by testosterone. This is the male hormone and of course it creates emotion and male drive but it was acting on a female mind, which had no counterbalance in oestrogen. Another clue was that I wondered during puberty why I wasn't growing breasts. It sounds immensely odd as it is one of the most ridiculous things to imagine, but it's true!

So here I am, happily married with a lovely daughter, running through life without realising my true nature. This is a miracle in some ways, as any major crack in the facade created by the mind would have probably killed me. Every so often during those years part of your mind tells you that you are female but you cannot understand what it is trying to say. This comes and goes and often gets suppressed for years but there comes a point when the energy to support and sustain that suppression goes. This is because your mind is lying to itself about what you are and you cannot keep that up for long. It uses such a large portion of your energy doing that without you even realising. Eventually the mind says, 'I am going to be me, regardless of what you think,' which is essentially what happened to me about five years ago.

I have to digress here to an accident I suffered in the mid nineties that in hindsight had an incredible influence on what later occurred. I learned to ride when I was forty and have an absolute love of horses. When out on a sponsored ride for charity I had one of those innumerable falls that riders have and I rolled in a particular manner with my head and shoulders hitting the ground first. Due to the nature of the fall, I damaged my brain by effectively splitting it in two; the rolling action of the impact somehow impaired most of the connections that form the bridge between the left and right side of the mind.

There were some amazing effects from this accident. Firstly, after the fall I sat in the lorry with my partner. She was obviously wondering if I was OK. I thought I was, but I explained to her that I had no idea how to drive home in terms of geography. I knew where I was and did not seem to be concussed. I could remember how to drive, but she had to tell me the way home. I drove the lorry all the way back to the yard, which was about an hour and a half away. I switched the diesel off, stepped out of the lorry and collapsed. I was carted off to the local hospital where they did all the appropriate tests for concussion. I was rational and my vision wasn't out of focus so I was discharged, though they didn't seem to know what was wrong with me at the time. Having arrived home I spent the next forty-eight hours in a time loop asking what year it was and if my pony was safe. After that time I remember suddenly coming round and saying, 'I think I knocked myself out again.' Not surprising given this was about the seventh time in my life I had done this! This time I could not remember how to go anywhere and it took two weeks of building up a mental map for me to be able to drive to work. I found I couldn't do my normal job at the Air Traffic Centre, as I seemed to have lost the ability to move information from short-term to long-term memory. Anything longer than twenty minutes would go, but strangely I could still remember everything to do with work itself, such as all my air traffic control knowledge and the associated technical systems.

When I returned the first thing people said was, 'Glad to have you back; about that twenty pounds you owe me...' because they all knew what had happened. Air traffic is a wonderful environment; it's a great family. We all laughed about it. But it became impossible for me to manage people. I could be walking down the corridor and I would forget what I was doing. My GP realised what had happened and said that I must not be in a stressed environment or else the neurones in my brain would rebuild the connections with the stress locked in. The company was opening a new air traffic facility and due to my computer expertise and the fact I lived relatively nearby it seemed sensible to put me into a new environment. Over the years my brain gradually healed itself but with certain physical limitations on the left side as though certain actions were being deliberately blocked.

Returning to the subject in hand, the actual nature of the transition from one gender to another is a very difficult concept to understand unless you have been through it. It consists of various stages, some of which happen sequentially and others simultaneously. The main thing first of all in my journey was I felt wrong in my body. I dieted for a year and lost two and a half stone; I wasn't that heavy to begin with so it was a huge change. I think I went from ten and a half to about eight stone. I didn't know why I was doing it; there was no way to explain it. The nearest I can imagine it being to is anorexia, which seems to be something that predominately affects the female mind, rather than the male.

My memory of the first part of the transition is lost as my mind rebuilt itself in the process. Essentially at the age of fifty-four everything started to slow and my brain began to shut down until there was hardly anything left. I was entirely clear in my mind but unable to hold conversations for any length of time. It was a bit like closing an operating system in a computer; the applications shut down, as if it was going into sleep mode. I couldn't see it but others could – although a sense of privacy prevented anyone asking me detailed questions because it was assumed that I was ill. It wouldn't have done any good because until you ask those questions of yourself as a transgendered individual you wouldn't know the answers anyway. When I asked my question, no one was more surprised than I was!

I got to the stage where I somehow knew that I was female, but how did I properly find out? At this point I decided to experiment with myself. I knew I needed to find the answer – in fact it was imperative that I found it. I decided to take oestrogen, the female hormone, by wearing patches. Although my professional career has been as an air traffic controller and computer system specialist, I was originally a scientist, having read geology at university. Because of my scientific disposition, and my cautious nature, I thought the safest way of obtaining an oestrogen source was to get some wild yam. This is plant oestrogen and is around five-hundredth of the strength of what you might consider artificial oestrogen – the kind prescribed by doctors. The general consensus among those who are transgendered was that the effect of herbal compounds was minimal and they took months for any observable effect to take place – in other words, it was ideal for me.

The wild yam arrived in the form of patches and after a day or two I finally plucked up courage to put one of the patches on at about four in the afternoon and thought no more about it. At eight minutes past two the next morning I was blown apart. I was locked rigid and I felt a massive surge of unknown energy start in my lower body, run through my torso to the nape of my neck and release straight into my brain. I tried to stop it and couldn't, realising that whatever it was, was somehow correct. This repeated eight times taking about two hours and that was it, I was all female, all switched on correctly and the male side was switched off. It was fantastic; the most wonderful feeling in the world. I had found the answer. I was female. Apparently the plant oestrogen had acted like a catalyst and it literally felt like one half of my mind was overwhelming the other. That was the female side of my mind that had been dormant all that time, but the oestrogen set it free and had taken it over. I think my aforementioned accident was essential in allowing this to happen. In fact a lot of people thought that the accident caused it all, but I know it didn't as with the current understanding of myself everything is crystal clear and all the events make perfect sense. I pictured it at the time as though I was starting an immense journey, one that I couldn't turn back on. It was as if I was leaving a harbour in New York and setting sail for Ireland, not in a liner, but a small yacht. I knew I was going to do an Atlantic crossing, but I had no idea what was going to happen on the way. After a period of time I finally plucked up courage and informed my wife Ann, who was amazingly understanding; she is immensely intelligent and very pragmatic. Her exact words were simply, 'Are you sure?' I knew I was. She is a remarkable lady and we have been together for thirty-six years. She then asked if I needed surgery, at which point I didn't know. It must have been an intense shock to her and I consider her one of the most compassionate individuals in the world. Her support and understanding has been crucial to my surviving the transition. The hardest part of the whole process is not the transformation in yourself, that part is beautiful and a fabulous experience, but rather its effect on those around you. A lot of relationships with people, even those who I had known for years, have been completely destroyed. When you embark on the journey you really put every relationship you've ever had on the line.

At this point, my partner quite rightly told me I really should go and see my GP. I wrote to him asking if I could come and see him about Gender Identity Disorder, although that is now an obsolete term. Having got my appointment I went in and he told me to sit down and explain it all to him. I said that it might be easier to show him as after just two months certain aspects of obvious female anatomy were appearing in all the right places! I explained what I had experienced, told him about the dieting and he just looked at me, burst out laughing, grinned and said, 'My goodness, as far as I am aware you are the first person in the world to correctly identify yourself, diagnostically, one hundred per cent with Gender Identity Disorder. Well done!' He explained why I ticked all the boxes and the key was that the oestrogen had the effect it did. Normally, it quite simply doesn't do anything much on a conventional male individual.

He explained that the reason is genetic; it is a bit like having one green eye and one blue eye. You can't do anything about it – it's you. He said that if I hadn't done what I did, in a year's time I would have been seriously ill and it would have been a mental illness which would have been caused from suppressing it. Therefore I had actually done the right thing.

Due to the fact that the changes were occurring at incredibly low doses of plant oestrogen, he took a few of the patches I had been using and sent them off to the pathology lab for analysis, to see if there was anything else in them that could have had a bearing on my physical changes. The patches came back a couple of weeks later and they were pure wild yam from Mexico with nothing else in them. He told me to carry on using them as my body was taking the plant oestrogen and transforming it into the type of oestrogen I needed to drive me. He said I seemed to have stepped beyond all medical knowledge as he and his colleagues had done some research and couldn't find a case like mine anywhere in the world.

My GP didn't want to put me through the health system because I was not ill and out of sheer interest every specialist would want to pull me to bits to find out how and why. I seemed to be controlling it from my mind; it was nothing to do with the other physical aspects of my body and was in his view quite incredible and more akin to a spiritual journey. So he sent me away, told me to carry on, see what happened from day to day and not to believe anything others told me but just discover it for myself. So I did!

What happened next was incredible. I do not know if anyone else has experienced the same – I suspect not. In January 2006 I started behaving more emotionally than I had been and it was as though my mind had gone back to the age of twelve. So there I was as an adult, doing my job, but the core of my mind was bouncing and dancing around as a twelve-year-old. I accelerated forward in time inside my mind about ten times faster than normal and went through puberty again, but this time, as a girl. I owe a great debt to all my female friends at work as they realised what was happening and helped me through this phase.

I started experiencing symptoms of a female cycle, but I obviously didn't have the same internal anatomy. My GP told me it was all done through my mind as the actual cycles themselves are controlled by the brain, but are amplified by the rest of the body. I was driving it all off five-hundredth of the normal hormone levels, so I am essentially 500 times more sensitive to hormones than a 'normal' human being. Even at the correct doses it still usually takes transgendered people two to three years, sometimes longer, to undergo the physical changes relevant to them.

In a way I had it easy, as although my body started to wage war on itself over the next year as the hormones fought at least I knew exactly what was going on. For someone who is in the middle in terms of gender it is far harder to come to terms with, but I was black and white: I knew I was female. At Easter 2006 I actually decided for sure that I was going to have an operation to become completely female as I felt there really was no other option. I had to wait until 24 January 2007 for an operation slot with a doctor in Thailand who was recommended to me. This was Dr Sanguan Kunaporn and his team at the Phuket International Hospital. I was told he had one of the best techniques for male to female surgery and I consider him and his staff some of the kindest and most understanding individuals I have ever come across.

In autumn 2006 I had a dry-run in a sense with surgery as I had to have my nose reshaped. The facial features that differ between men and women work as very subtle visual clues. My nose was rather misshapen due to a previous fall off a horse and was not very feminine. I was recommended Mr Musgrove in Manchester, who is a leading expert in altering gender-related features.

He told me that not only was he confident that he could adjust my nose but that it was actually broken and I had not been breathing properly through one side for quite some time. He quickly slotted me in for an operation, the result was one beautiful new nose that worked correctly and I am eternally grateful for the skill and expertise that created it.

Sadly, finance does play a large role in a successful transition. There is very little public money available to help those who cannot afford the procedures. Whilst I elected to have my nose-job in the UK, it would have been five times more expensive to go through with the full transgender procedure here in the UK or the USA than in Thailand. Luckily Thailand is where most of the research to do with the operations happens because, in Thai culture, transgendered people are entirely accepted. The Thai people instinctively treat you as an individual, which is something that sadly does not happen in the West. I am so glad I went through the procedure in an accepting environment.

I really haven't much to say about the actual surgical procedure as most people seem to have seen it on television. The really fun bit was sorting out the size of breast augmentation I needed as certain aspects of the front did need a bit of enhancement. This consisted of trying various sizes to see what looked best – all I will say is that a sense of proportion is required and the results are beautiful and not all silicon! My miracle was coming round and finding that nothing hurt at all. I really didn't need painkillers. The medical staff viewed this as quite exceptional. The actual stay in hospital was about two weeks – the hardest part was being in bed and not being allowed to move for three whole days. I had a wonderful, if very quiet, recuperation at a hotel at the northern end of Patong Beach. I flew home business class and was met at Heathrow by my colleague Andy from work, who was amazed at how well I looked.

A very hard part of the process for me, and I think common for all transgendered individuals, is the intense self-doubt that can occur, which is hugely exacerbated by the people who see you as a freak. During the long process you have to face yourself but it is far harder facing the world. Changing gender is a very hard concept for people to wrap their minds around and it is incredibly destabilising for everyone. But the very few people who saw me for what I really am made me shine. I can best illustrate this by looking at the two extremes of perception. The intensely sad end is people who I have known for years and yet they are so terrified that they have chosen to cut me off completely and will not even communicate with my partner. These lost friendships are the hardest part of the whole journey but it is entirely understandable in retrospect, as it seems to be an underlying fear shared by many. A young lady at work who had survived cancer explained it to me beautifully. Nobody would talk to her about it, because they were afraid. Similarly with me, people don't know what to say because they have no understanding of it; you are undertaking a journey that they can't comprehend. Some people literally hate you for it. They often don't understand why, but in a sense you are reflecting things back that they don't understand about themselves.

The other end is perhaps best illustrated by my daughter Elizabeth who had the immense courage to come to Thailand with me. She didn't have to do this but volunteered on the grounds that I shouldn't have to go alone, which I would have been otherwise. This was quite remarkable because I had already turned her life upside-down from it all. She told me afterwards she was so very worried for me, the odd thing being that I had no worries at all – I knew I would be fine! Early in my journey we drifted apart as neither of us could communicate. We were both afraid we had lost each other, but in fact we have gained each other. She understands why I had to do what I did to become me although our relationship is of course different. That is the beauty that shines out of the entire journey like a lighthouse.

The middle ground is where the vast majority sit. In hindsight I know I was probably annoying everyone just by being me but there is not a lot one can do about it. Although it is apparently a very unusual event for most people, as I went on I discovered more and more individuals who had met or knew someone who was friends with a transgendered individual. I don't know how many of us there really are as most like to live their lives privately and just enjoy being themselves. People told me I was immensely brave but I don't know why – how can one be brave just by being oneself?

Looking back it is like I have a set of memories, but the emotions that go with them no longer exist. They can't do because I am not male – I am female. The mind itself has essentially thrown away all emotion and memory to do with being male. The person who arrives after you've changed gender is the real person. Being transgendered has been treated as a mental illness over the years, hence the word 'disorder'. Unfortunately it can appear that way because lots of people can't deal with it all. You have to be immensely resilient to get through it; transgendered people are the most resilient people in the world – they have to be. We have survived one of the hardest journeys it is possible for a human being to take. You have to go to the core of yourself, recognise that you are a complete and utter fraud, then find yourself, rebuild yourself from nothing and, if that isn't hard enough, you've then got to take on the whole world.

Just prior to my operation I spoke at length with a colleague and good friend of mine about my situation and I explained to him that I was stuck inside my own body. He understood and said the most wonderful thing, 'You are your own twin aren't you?!' It got me thinking and one evening driving home from work the revelation felt like a thunderbolt in my mind. Of course I am my own twin; I am an internal twin. I actually have a real left and right side of the brain but in fact the female side of me has taken over and the male side has left. The same friend also came up with a fantastic analogy for my situation. He said, 'You know it's incredible, I have known you for twenty years. It is like you have written the male side of your life on a sheet of A4 paper and as far as we knew, that was correct. But now it is as though you have turned it over and you are writing on the other side as a girl and if you hold it to the light, it's magic, it's like two in one. That's why you are a twin inside.' I think that is a great way to explain it.

One of the most beautiful parts of the journey is the point at which you must decide to live in the other gender. In my case this was at Easter 2006. At this point you legally have to change identity and one of the best parts is deciding what your own name is going to be. My name before was Simon and I always gently laugh at myself and say I changed it to Siobhan because it saved a great deal of hassle; I didn't have to change my signature for a start! Actually, though, names are incredibly important when it comes to changing gender. I chose Siobhan because it had such an intense Celtic resonance to it and I am Irish at heart. My partner, daughter and those family and friends that I can still talk to use the nickname Si, which is fine, and I can live with that.

One of the hardest parts for people who have known you before seems to be the change to the new name and using the correct gender pronoun. It takes around two years for someone to cope with it, I have found. People can't do it immediately and that's partly why they get so completely destabilised. Although they can visually see you being dressed as a female they retain a mental image of you as male, which is then turned on its head. People don't mean to cause offence, but if someone accidentally called me Simon, it would hurt so much; it would hurt to my core. Even now after everything I have gone through, it really strikes a chord if people get it wrong. I know people don't mean it, it is just a habit, but it comes over as an incredible feeling of disrespect in the sense of, 'Why can't you be bothered to get my name right?'

I have been helped over this by an old friend from university who teaches English and is an expert in the differences in the way girls and boys learn. She told me not to worry about the names and explained that because language is embedded in the brain and is so linked to vision people can't help it. Names and the gender pronoun are so powerful that even if they wish to say 'she' or 'Siobhan' they can't do it. Because normally individuals don't have to rationally think about names and genders, it just flows straight out of the subconscious. This shows you the depths that one has to go to change gender.

The UK is one of the few countries in the world that recognises transgendered people correctly and actually states that it is nothing to do with mental illness and is everything to do with genetics. I am afraid that a lot of countries still treat transgendered individuals under what is called the 'Harry Benjamin guidelines', which relate far more to the psychiatric and medical views and nothing to do with the individual. Worse still, some countries have no understanding at all and this leads to the most appalling state for some individuals where they stand no chance of becoming themselves.

Specific research has been done to try and determine why transgendered people exist by utilising magnetic resonance imaging of the brain. A valid test group of males, females and male to female transgendered individuals had various photographs presented to them whilst in a MRI scanner. The females' minds reacted one way, the males reacted in another and all the transgendered people reacted in the opposite of what they were physically, so in other words, their minds were female. This has prompted further research as an apparent mechanism is now believed to have been found.

In humans all foetuses start out as female and then differentiate into male and female as appropriate to the X and Y chromosomes. At fifteen weeks, in the womb, there is a burst of testosterone and effectively the organs and structure for a boy start to form. At around twenty-eight to thirty weeks there is a second burst of testosterone and, if it's a boy, the mind develops specific male characteristics. I was a twin born ten weeks premature but unfortunately my twin died just after birth so I have nobody to compare myself with. I surmised that my condition was because I was born early but realised that didn't add up because if that were true, all boys born very premature would be transgendered and obviously they're not. So there was still a piece of the puzzle missing.

That missing piece seems to have been found by Australian researchers. On a DNA strand there is sometimes an immensely rare section that differs from the norm and basically, if you have it, when that second burst of testosterone occurs it masks the mind from the effects so you end up with a female mind in a male body. That is male to female transgender, but I think it is much more sensitive in me because I was born early.

The discovery has led to some new analysis and it's now thought that perhaps around one in 30,000 people around the world have the 'masking' genetic structure. It doesn't seem to dominate in any particular regions and is spread randomly across the world. It may seem that it appears more in certain native cultures, but that is because it is more accepted. The questions are: why does it exist? What's it doing? Why doesn't it disappear if it serves no purpose? These are the questions I felt I had to ask. The one aspect that you have no understanding of until it emerges is one's own sexuality, which cannot emerge fully until all aspects of being yourself in gender terms are stable.

People have asked me if, having changed gender, I am now a lesbian. This is a perfectly natural question as that would seem to be the rational viewpoint and best illustrated by the House of Lords, who created the appropriate legislation. When I receive my Gender Identity Certificate I am officially female and my Birth Certificate is changed accordingly. This means I have never been male and I have therefore never been married. Thus I have to change to a Civil Partnership to keep the same legal relationship with my partner.

I am now completely female with all the appropriate apparatus and I find it all absolutely fabulous. I have great fun being me and being female as it is the first time in my life when I have not been at war with my own body. But now I have no inclination sexually either way. I feel absolutely balanced and I am, in sexual terms, what would be considered androgynous with no interest whatsoever in either sex. This very balance has unlocked a whole new dimension of 'being', which is the strangest aspect of all.

To explore this part I have to delve into something that is called metaphysics. This is the word used to describe the nature of alternative realities but in my case it is based on the nature of my experiences crossing the gender divide. The mind has two sides, one of which may be termed 'rational', from which the ego stems, and the other 'non-rational', which is intuitive. Einstein postulated that problems created in one side of the mind could only be resolved in the other side. Every mind has both sides but it appears to be very difficult for people to go between the two sides easily. It is possible to break down the barriers between the sides but unfortunately from the rational perspective this can only occur through intense trauma or a life-changing experience. I suppose mine might be considered a massive life-changing experience!

A lot of the experiences in the mind associated with my journey have been entirely unexpected. I was essentially a logical and rational left-brained individual before but have had to add all the mental capabilities to the right non-rational side of my mind. I never knew these existed and have had to come to terms with them by accepting and trying not to explain them rationally. The most obvious one is associated with questions I asked about the initial surge of energy that allowed me to really be me. I described this to a friend who said, 'you have blown all your chakras open! Have a look at this site on the net.' Since I had never heard the term I went online, looked and found she was right! To gain further insight I found a beautiful book called *Eastern Body, Western Mind*, which tied together the views on psychology from the Western viewpoint with that of the Eastern tradition. This proved immensely useful in balancing what I had experienced physically into a mental picture that I could cope with.

In the autumn of 2006, before I went to Thailand, I found that for some reason people kept coming up and wanting to talk to me. I could not understand this until I went to a Mind Body Spirit event and was told by several of the participants that I had a healing energy, which was very unusual. I had no idea until then that this was possible and I certainly didn't consider myself a healer. I now understand after a lot of questioning and with hindsight that this was essentially what is called a shamanic journey, where the individual goes within themselves then up and out into a connection to the spiritual. The nature of this journey is best explained by specific events that are key to my understanding of it and are all validated by others. This is vital as only external validation with no prior reference by oneself is relevant; otherwise it would originate in ego.

The first key event occurred in the summer of 2008 when I met a lovely Japanese lady called Yoko on Glastonbury Tor. To cut a long story short, my friend Sue was invited to Singapore by Yoko to do tarot readings and she wondered if I would like to go too. Something came into my mind saying it was essential that I go, so I agreed and booked my flight. A month before we went, Yoko's husband Osama asked whether we would be interested in going to a conference involving feng shui that his engineering firm was sponsoring. It seemed intriguing, so I agreed.

The conference, held at Singapore University in December 2008, was about the structure of buildings, their surroundings and associated energy flows. However odd it seems from a Western viewpoint, this is essential from a Chinese cultural perspective and is all part of normal planning practice. Sue and I were treated as honoured guests and considered part of the conference, which was remarkable for us to start with as neither of us understood a thing about it! After the initial photographs there was a morning tea break. As soon as I walked into the room, one of the girls made eye contact and seemed to make an immediate connection with me, but I had no idea why. She came straight over and asked in Mandarin if someone would please act as an interpreter. Through the interpreter she said, 'Do you realise what you are? You're bringing in the chi energy from the outer realms into this world; you're a feng shui master!'

I confess I was completely baffled by this as I didn't know anything about feng shui! However, over the course of the conference I gradually came to realise what they were seeing in me. They said that in their energy terms my right side was male and my left side was female, and that it could be seen in my eyes. They thought it was fantastic, even though I couldn't understand any of it myself. The conference continued and eventually light dawned when I was told I had achieved complete calm and was perfectly balanced, like the yin-yang symbol. It was certainly not what I expected but I feel immensely privileged to be allowed to refer to myself as 'The White Tigress with the Blue Dragon'. The White Tigress refers to my year of birth and the Blue Dragon refers to the quality of the energy I bring from the Chinese perspective.

The second key sequence of events began with a suggestion in August 2008 that I might like to attend a Mind Body Spirit event in San Francisco in October of that year. Again there was this feeling that it was essential I go. Whilst doing my travel planning, I realised I could do something I really loved – a transcontinental rail journey. This was a wonderful experience and much the best way to travel. Also San Francisco itself is very safe for someone like me and I felt really at home there. I met various individuals who gradually made me realise that I was appearing to them as the equivalent of a Native American medicine woman. As with the Chinese experience I had no cultural links or understanding at the time of what this actually meant.

The third key event, which unified the first two, occurred in April 2009 in Glastonbury. My friend Yvonne-Anne organises psychic and craft fairs and just prior to the April event I had finally given in to spiritual promptings, which seemed more like kickings. I bought for myself a beautiful Cheyenne war bonnet that seemed to be needed to acknowledge the male side of myself. Yvonne-Anne said she felt I should wear my Native American garb, so I donned everything for the occasion. At the event was an aura photographer called Tonya and her partner who both had connections with the Indian culture – Tonya herself being Cherokee-German.

When they first saw me the same thing happened with the Chinese in that again it was as though particular connections had been made that I didn't understand. It was explained to me that my war bonnet was entirely appropriate as the symbolism associated with it was unity between all the races and also that I was a 'Twin Spirit' in nature. Native Americans have apparently had a natural diet high in oestrogen over a long period of time. Native American males do not grow beards. This has resulted in a natural inclination in both genders to have a testosterone and oestrogen balance that is unique to the culture. Also there is a greater prevalence of individuals who are referred to as 'Twin Spirit' and shamans. They were both intrigued by me and asked if I had ever had an aura photograph taken. I hadn't.

Aura photography is now based on digitally processed biofeedback. I had not considered it of any relevance before but my own feedback indicated a balance of energy with all the chakras at the same level and an absolutely flat line for a state of calm. The photograph produced a beautiful gold aura. A couple of hours later in the middle of a conversation with Tonya, I felt a massive flow of energy and apparent heat, which I associate with a concept of 'confirmation of truth'. I asked if we could repeat the photograph whilst in this state and two remarkable results were seen. The chakras were completely different with a massive increase in the lower chakra indicating 'grounding' and an increase in energy of twenty-five per cent. The photograph was amazing and, incredibly, either side of the median bodyline were completely different colours. Tonya exclaimed, 'My goodness, male one side and female the other! Perfect Twin Spirit!'

This was quite incredible as it independently matched the Chinese view exactly but from a completely different cultural perspective. The Chinese professor had told me they view this energy as universal and those who can handle it have 'Sincerity of Being'.

So where has my journey taken me to and what have the effects been? If I hadn't had my transgender operation in January 2007, I do not think I would have lasted another six months. I would have been dead, literally worn out by my body pulling itself apart with the battle between the hormones raging inside me. The experience had to be accepted though as that is the nature of spirituality; accepting whatever is thrown at you. Accepting it saved me. In retrospect the physical side of the operation was the easy bit for me. It was fantastic coming round, and not needing painkillers was incredible. That is the spiritual aspect of it. None of it ever hurt because it was me.

My face is virtually female now because my mind is now free and has managed to put it all back where it should be. My body has been blown back to the apparent medical age of forty-five. I have the knowledge of having been alive for nearly sixty years but mentally I am in my early twenties because the core of my mind has rebuilt itself. It has come from about the age of twelve to early twenties in three years.

All transgendered people go through an amazing journey and must be given the deepest respect for it. All transgendered people are totally unique and you can't put any of us into a box. That's the one thing you can't do; we have worked so hard not to be trapped again.

I think generally all transgendered people who go through the whole process are immensely happy. They sparkle and bounce, as everything is new. I consider myself to have now arrived in my harbour from my Atlantic crossing and with it I now have my 'moral compass'. This has just three rules; 'nothing must be hidden', 'harm no one' and 'do what you must'.

The experience has been one of intense happiness together with incredible sadness and I consider myself one of the most privileged individuals in the world to have been able to complete this journey across the gender divide. The journey itself has been a combination of the physical, mental and spiritual, and in hindsight can really only be treated as a holistic 'whole'.

Life is unique, connected and is a beautiful balance. It has taken me nearly sixty years to learn the power of balance. I am lucky to have been not only born again, but born into a set of memories. If you find even a little inspiration from my story then that is just wonderful.

I have had to handle all of it; cope with everybody's opinion, cope with the world, understand how to be female and overcome a catalogue of obstacles to get to where I am today. And if someone were to ask me if I would do it all again given the chance? Then yes, of course I would.

# MATTHEW WOOD-HILL...

## ... ON SURVIVING PROLONGED EXPOSURE TO CARBON MONOXIDE

'We had been exposed to the carbon monoxide emitted from the gas heater for about eight long hours... The utter helplessness of being unable to sit up by myself, and then attempting to stand (with someone's help) but feeling my legs collapse beneath me, was extreme, a kind of powerlessness I'd never felt before and have not felt since.'

When you hear horror stories of people's gap year trips, when you hear warnings from your friends and family, you just put it down to paranoia and think, 'it'll never happen to me,' but the truth is, as I regrettably found out, that such incidents can happen at any time to any one of us.

The start to my six-month stay in South America had been two weeks of misery; I was alone, thousands of miles from home and living with an Ecuadorian family, whom I struggled to communicate with. I had broken up with my then girlfriend at the airport as I left and my only source of real company was a forty-five-year-old Canadian on the same volunteer programme who, if truth be told, I felt unable to connect with. Such emotions, as an eighteen-year-old, who had invested much time and money in the months ahead, were difficult to deal with.

I had felt like I was making little headway in my role as an English language teacher in the primary school in Quito, so I resolved to use my second free weekend to get away from the city and my troubles and turn things around. Wandering through La Mariscal, the main backpacker street of Quito, had become something of a habit, with the frequency of my visits to various Internet cafes bordering on the obsessive. A particular one-day tour to Volcan Cotopaxi, the perfectly formed snow-capped cone of a volcano, featured in the window of one travel agency had really caught my eye.

The tour, for a mere $50, looked fantastic; a ride atop the roof of a train into the national park, followed by a jeep ride as far up the volcano as vehicles were permitted; once there, a hike up to the snow line and a chance to see one of the glaciers up close. Then to top it all off, a stunning descent of the volcano by mountain bike. This was the kind of exhilarating experience I had been dreaming of for the past year while planning my trip and it brought back the cheer and enthusiasm that had been missing from the previous couple of weeks. As if all that was not reason enough, the woman at the agency, apparently desperate for me to commit myself, offered a free night's lodging in their hacienda, just on the outskirts of the national park. How could I refuse an offer like that?

The setting was perfect. After a long and tiring day of hiking and cycling at altitude the hacienda was more than a welcome retreat, if a little cold. It was precisely for this reason that, aided by a Texan girl called Tina, I attempted to figure out how to light the heater in my room. It was a dormitory in an outbuilding that I was sharing with just one other person; Wataru, from Japan, who the guides, somewhat racially, called 'Suzuki' for practicality. Tina kindly lent us some matches and we were now confident that we would at least not freeze to death that evening.

So around midnight, having spent a relaxed evening meeting new people in the hacienda, and finally doing what I was expecting to be doing on my gap year, I headed to bed, having arranged to meet several of the other guests for breakfast at around 8 a.m.

And here is where the trail ends, as it were. Or at least here is where my memory ceases to remain an active part of the story. What follows are the events I have attempted to piece together according to the intermittent fragments of my own consciousness and, more largely, the sequence of events as recounted by those who witnessed them.

Like the dangers associated with gap-year travel, which in reality are few and far between, the risks of exposure to gas were not something I would have paid a great deal of attention to. Indeed, only recently when I was in my university's housing office was the magnitude of my own situation, and the good fortune by which I escaped unscathed, brought home once again. 'Carbon monoxide poisoning,' it read, 'could result in brain damage, coma, or death.'

Going to bed that night in Ecuador I had noticed a difference in my breathing – by now the heater had already been on for a couple of hours – but I put it down to a long day and the altitude. Perhaps it was naivety, perhaps stupidity, on my part not to turn the heater off before bed. Nevertheless, as far as I was concerned there was no real reason to be worried.

When it came to breakfast time, our absence was noted; when you're meeting new people all the time you can forgive a little tardiness. Suspicions were aroused when a girl in the room next to us described hearing 'strange noises' and 'screams' coming from our room in the night. Knocking on the door was met with no answer and, when the door was finally opened, both Wataru and I were discovered 'unresponsive'. We had been exposed to the carbon monoxide emitted from the gas heater for about eight long hours. We were then lifted outside by three people each and laid on the grass at the front of the building, presumably in little but our underwear. I had lost all circulation from the waist down and I can distinctly remember the horrible feeling of paralysis when I later awoke in hospital, unable to move my limbs or to lift my neck. Having been clothed we were taken by jeep to a nearby toll where an ambulance was waiting.

On the way there, however, I was still 'unresponsive', no pupil dilations, nothing. It was at that point, Tina told me, I had stopped breathing. This really got to me. To be told that was one of the hardest things I've ever had to hear. I was unconscious throughout.

I woke up, slowly recovered my strength and was left feeling pretty terrible. To be told I had stopped breathing and that she had to unblock my airway and administer mouth-to-mouth resuscitation was really quite scary.

I am forever indebted to her, and without her skills as a medical student I might not be alive today. So having just about been kept alive this far I was put into the ambulance and given an oxygen mask. The ambulance was then able to take me as far as the outskirts of Quito; for whatever reasons this ambulance (perhaps all ambulances) were not allowed into the city, so I was transferred back into the jeep. It was during this second spell in the jeep that I finally regained consciousness. The small parts I recall of this journey to the hospital were chiefly: struggling to swallow the Gatorade that was being tipped into my mouth, not being able to move my head (or any other part of my body for that matter) and being unable to utter anything other than a long, deep throaty growl in response to questions I was being asked.

I drifted in and out of consciousness for I don't know how long until I woke up in a hospital bed, again drifting in and out of sleep. Here I was given more oxygen and attempts were made to give me an IV drip. The efforts to locate a suitable vein were evidently unsuccessful on the first few occasions – even though I was under the impression that this was one of the first things you learned in med school and it made me question exactly whose hands my lifeless body was left in. When I did eventually begin to recover and sustain my consciousness I found I was covered in obscure prick marks from these attempts as well as, most alarmingly, being unable to move.

As I understand it, the carbon monoxide molecules bind tightly to the haemoglobin in the red blood cells, starving the muscles and vital organs of oxygen and slowly shutting the body down completely. The utter helplessness of being unable to sit up by myself, and then attempting to stand (with someone's help) but feeling my legs collapse beneath me, was extreme, a kind of powerlessness I'd never felt before and have not felt since.

I wanted to cry, but my body, or perhaps my pride, wouldn't let me.

I recovered speedily and, upon finally regaining some feeling in my legs by the middle of the afternoon, I was able to change out of Wataru's clothes, which I had been dressed in (his trousers were especially tight) and into my own before leaving the hospital at around 4 p.m. – only eight hours after the situation had seemed critical. I was probably in no fit state to leave the hospital and had this happened in the UK I am certain I would have been kept in overnight at the very least. However, as soon as I had gained a bit of strength back I was desperate to leave. I suppose I had felt violated by the strange marks that had been inflicted on my numb body and very detached from the whole ordeal. Even now it feels like someone else's story, in part due to the fact that I had to have my own story read back to me at the time because I was such an inactive participant. It did not escape me, however, just how close I came to death; how another thirty minutes might have been the difference between irreparable damage, or worse. How if I had chosen to go to bed earlier that night I may never have woken up the next morning. Was I in the wrong? Surely there should have been signs warning of the dangers of the heater? And did I put Wataru in danger? He recovered quicker than I did, thankfully, though I never saw him again once he left the hospital.

It was impossible to convey over the phone to my parents what I had been through and to put them at ease about everything. They offered to buy me a flight home, knowing what a torrid time my first fortnight had been, and it was only at that point and after all I had experienced that I learned that I was not a quitter. The profound impact of this event, above all, was that for the remaining months in South America I had no regrets and I truly did live every day as if it were my last.

# VALERIE AUSTIN...

## ... ON THE AMNESIA THAT TRANSFORMED HER LIFE

---

*'It came down to the fact that I only had a twenty-four-hour memory. I would have forgotten yesterday and tomorrow, I would forget today. I no longer had a broken heart since I didn't even remember I had been in love.'*

---

I was overworked; I had just come out of a love affair and was making a lot of money at something I really disliked when I had the car accident that completely changed my life. I lost my memory. But it hadn't begun there. That was just the catalyst.

It was a sunny day in autumn – I must have been around twenty-four. I was laughing with my mother in the private quarters of our hotel. We were just about to dash out and have a drink with my new boyfriend. It was that heady time when you are very excited to see the new love in your life. The summer was over so the hotel only had a handful of guests staying.

I suddenly turned round to see my ex-husband walk in. In those few seconds I wondered why he was there as he had a court order to prevent him coming anywhere near me. Not because he was violent but due to his actions. When we separated he had twice attempted to kidnap our son, breaking down doors and threatening to take him abroad. I was beside myself with worry. I will always wonder if it was the court order that caused him to snap but, on reflection, I don't see what else I could have done.

On that day, with the blue skies and excitement in the air from my new life of freedom, he walked straight past me and all our lives changed forever. He said to my mother in a strange voice, 'It's all your fault!'

Then he lunged at her and started to strangle her. I remember the look on his face; without a doubt his intention was to kill her. I was looking at a stranger, not the man I once knew and loved.

It happened in a flash. My mind was trying to fathom it all. This could not be happening; I must be dreaming. My ex-husband was very strong but had never been violent towards his family. I looked round for something to hit him with to save my mother. I spotted a letter-opener in the shape of a large knife and a very heavy stand-up astray. I didn't use either of them. This decision has haunted me ever since. Why didn't I use them? Was I a coward? Could I have saved my mother from the terrible injuries she suffered if I had just stabbed him or knocked him unconscious? These questions were to be answered more than thirty years later.

I quickly ran to the hotel's bar a short distance away and grabbed a wine bottle. When I returned, my ex-husband was smashing my mother's head onto the TV. I hit him over the head as hard as I could with the wine bottle. This made him lunge at me. I ran to get help from the kitchen where the chef and his staff were. When we all reached the private

225

room, my ex-husband had dragged my mother onto the floor so he could jam his foot against the door, preventing it from opening. The chef was small but fearless. We all pushed at the door, it opened a little and the chef managed to slide in his fist. That few seconds gave him the opportunity to hit my ex-husband where it hurts. Subsequently he let go of my mother and with his guard down we all burst in. We were all occupied with trying to help my mother whilst he staggered out of the building, but not before throwing a chair through a window where the guests were dining. Dripping with blood from an injury he suffered whilst my mother was trying to defend herself, he simply walked away. The police picked him up not long afterwards, just walking in a daze; he hadn't even tried to hide.

I looked at my mother on the floor and there was so much blood. I thought she was dead. It looked like a murder scene; blood all over the place. It was on the floor, up the walls and the sideboard had about half a pint of blood on it. I was in so much shock that I just wandered about in a daze until the police arrived.

My mother recovered, if you can call it that, but we were all scarred forever. Life was never going to be the same; we all went through years of turmoil and guilt. Now I can speak about that day and the horror without getting emotional; there are no feelings. I know I should feel something but there is nothing – I suppose it is part of my self-preservation.

My son was eight and I had been married just over eight years. We were the glamorous couple that nobody thought would part. We met at college but neither of us knew that he would turn out to be the alcoholic gambler that would eventually wreck our marriage. We didn't know because, as students, we didn't have the money to find out.

I was an only child and my inheritance was to be the lovely hotel we owned. But everything had changed and my mother, understandably, found things very difficult. I felt guilty and ended up leaving home, the hotel, which I will always regret as I loved the life so much. From being a fairly shy girl in my marriage I became a strong and independent woman with a very high earning capacity. This was something I found out after joining a commission-only sales team. I was thrown in at the deep end of a very difficult cold-selling marketplace. I would be left in a town in the early morning somewhere in the UK and be picked up in the evening. My job was to go round to businesses selling advertising space, knocking on doors and canvassing the bosses or directors.

I worked at this for seven years and became the top sales person out of sixty others, even breaking sales records. Since I only needed to work four days a week I was able to take up various hobbies. I managed a pop group, had my own 'what's on' newspaper with a journalist friend and was going out with some wonderful men. One was a scientist and the other a film director. I was even invited onto various film sets around the country. Then out of the blue I met a detective and fell head over heels in love. I had a whirlwind romance that had just ended on that fateful night when I had my car accident.

I remember it being after midnight and there was no one on the motorway. I saw a person dash across the road. I swerved and ended up skidding into the side. I had a new convertible sports car each year due to my excessive mileage from travelling and because of my financial circumstances. I was very proud of my shiny MGB and I was a very good driver as I had been spending a lot of time driving all over the country. But now my car was completely out of control and bouncing through the shrubbery. I found out later that

I had knocked down three trees before plunging thirty feet into a ravine.

I can still remember being smashed against the car like a doll until I finally came to a stop. I believed I was going to die and I was waiting for the moment when I would be thrown through the window. This was in the 1970s before seat belts were made compulsory. In those days, even drinking and driving was not as severe a crime as it is today. I came to a stop as the car hit a barrier of some sort and, as miracles would have it, I didn't hit the windscreen; I have no idea why or how I defied gravity. However, the only part of my body that wasn't hurt was my face. Every other inch of me was in a badly bruised state.

I remember sitting in my car with the windscreen wipers going and very loud music still playing. I was wondering how badly I was injured and it all seemed very surreal.

I eased myself out and looked round to see how damaged my car was. In my dazed state I thought the car was OK but, in actual fact, it was a write-off. I climbed up the bushy ravine as I could hear the motorway at the top. I had no shoes on and must have looked as if I had been attacked. I walked onto the hard shoulder and attempted to flag someone down. Eventually a lorry stopped. He had seen headlights down in the bushes off the road and guessed that there had been an accident. He was my knight in shining armour. I then passed out.

I was only allowed to stay in hospital overnight, as nothing was broken. When I saw my local doctor he said I had almost reached the pearly gates. He said that the bruising was so bad on my back that he was surprised that I hadn't broken my neck.

It was a few weeks before I realised I had amnesia. You don't know you forget things until it is pointed out. I was recovering but I still couldn't work and walking was difficult. It took me fifteen minutes of sheer pain to get out of bed and the same amount of time to lie down. All my muscles were bruised and the pain was excruciating. Once I was up and about I was all right but getting there was agony.

It was my friends that noticed my memory problem first. I would not remember what had happened the night before. I would be constantly looking for things; I would lose my purse and find my keys and then end up looking for something else. This would wile away hours most days. My friends would come to meet me to go out but my hair would be wet still and I would have no idea where the time had gone.

It came down to the fact that I only had a twenty-four-hour memory. I would have forgotten yesterday and tomorrow, I would forget today. I no longer had a broken heart since I didn't even remember I had been in love.

I was unemployable and soon there was no money left. I couldn't continue my sales job as it depended on me knowing the roads. I could not remember anywhere. Everywhere I went it was as if I was there for the first time. I even forgot I played the guitar and it was as though all my music reading ability had just been wiped out. I was attractive with a good figure so found that I started getting marriage proposals. Men seemed to love the vulnerability that was synonymous with my memory loss.

I could walk out of a door and forget who I had been talking to. My memory was so bad that it started to seem insignificant to even watch TV, as I would forget it soon after. I started to wonder what the point of anything was. I wasn't so much depressed as frustrated.

I went for a week's holiday to Los Angeles with a friend and had an introduction to the international editor of *The*

*Hollywood Reporter*, John Austin. I also met the well-known TV personality Robin Leach, from *Lives of the Rich and Famous* and *Entertainment Tonight*. I subsequently married John a year later and moved to America and Robin wrote my story in *The Globe*, which was usually a scandal magazine but was good for me since it led to further publicity about what I had been through.

A hypnotherapist who lived in California invited me to go to one of his training sessions. He said he would cure me of my memory loss. He had read my story in the UK papers and said he would do it for free if I agreed to attend his course.

I remember the date because, as he worked with me, the secretary came in and said President Reagan had been shot. He regressed me to that fateful day in the hotel. I was at the point where I was questioning why I didn't use the letter knife or the heavy ashtray when he said, 'You didn't because you loved your ex-husband and your mother, so you were in conflict.' The next thing I knew my memory was back after two years of living without it.

My new life was very glamorous. I had married in Las Vegas on a press junket, honeymooned at the Cannes Film Festival, stayed at the famous Carlton, gone to the Oscars and other fabulous parties. Then, to top it all off, I had got my memory back. But my fully recovered memory only lasted a year until tragedy struck again. My father became senile following a fall onto concrete and my mother, who was now an invalid – depending entirely on him – died of a broken heart. It was too much and I lost my memory once again. This time around it was less severe as I had about a two-week memory span.

One day I left the US simply forgetting that I had a husband there. We later divorced and I became a journalist in the then bustling Fleet Street. I had so many contacts in the film industry that I found it easy to get interviews with celebrities. I wrote for magazines and had a couple of my own – *London People* and *Weekend People*. Then I suddenly decided I needed a change and got interested in hypnosis. With my varied experience I was very good at it and I soon became well known. I have since written five books and I focus on training people to practice hypnotherapy. It was because of my memory deficiency that I was able to understand the mind so well. I developed a method that I called 'The Austin Technique' that was like a mind map to get to the source of people's problems. It turned out to be very teachable.

In the last recession in the early 1990s I worked in Malaysia and became very well known from radio interviews, newspaper articles and regular TV appearances – so well known that I even had my own signature tune 'Smoke Gets in Your Eyes' as I was famous for the 'Stop Smoking in One Hour' therapy. In fact I coined the title and my book of the same name was published first in Malaysia and then in the UK. Others have copied the title but I developed the one-hour technique when it was thought to be impossible. It could take up to ten sessions of hypnosis before then.

I met husband number three in Indiana and have finally got it right. I have never got my full memory back but using hypnosis helps me function well on a day-to-day basis.

At my son's wedding a strange thing happened. I had a flashback and suddenly knew why I had not used the letter-knife or that heavy ashtray. I relived it. When I looked to choose a weapon to save my mother, in an instant, I realised the knife was blunt and wouldn't go through my husband's jacket, which would have given him time to attack me. The ashtray was so heavy that I may have missed him and hit my mother. But the worst part, when I relived the horrific moment through the flashback, was seeing the hate in his eyes as he turned to lunge at me. I then knew he was ready to kill me as well. I realised that my actions had probably saved us both. I was running for help not out of cowardice but because it was the only thing I could do. When someone loses it, like he did, it can take several policemen to pull them away. The truth did help me but I still wonder what it would be like to regain the exceptional memory that I had before.

The flashback was a turning point in my training. It gave me such an insight into the workings of the brain and how presumption can play a negative part in therapy. The hypnotist that had worked with me had just stopped too early in my case and didn't get to the ending. I didn't see what had really happened and I can tell you, at that point, I certainly didn't love my ex-husband, like he said I did. I believe if the therapist had gone further into that terrible happening, the truth would have come out and I would not have had a relapse of memory later.

My ex-husband was the first man in the UK to receive bail on attempted murder. The condition was that he had to stay with a relative in Scotland and sign into the police station every day. He later received a suspended sentence. He never did anything like that again. However, we all suffered psychologically. I struggled with my memory dysfunction, eventually my mother became bedridden and my ex-husband's life was ruined as well.

Although terrible, there is some positivity in this tragedy. I can now train hypnotherapists in a much more effective way when dealing with trauma. Through my books, particularly *Self-hypnosis* that I wrote whilst in Langkawi, Malaysia, I am very proud of the people that I have trained. Over the past twenty years I have trained many therapists worldwide and they are out there helping thousands of people at this moment. I could almost say that my horror has had a positive ending; it has helped so many others.

# LAWRENCE FORD...

## ... ON HIS BONE-SHATTERING ARM WRESTLE

*'The bone had snapped and shards of it were visible, it was a spiral break right down the length of the bone. I saw that there were two sharp bits desperately trying to protrude through the skin... I muttered a few words of shock and surprise.'*

I was at university in Southampton. It was the first week of my last year. During this time I was sharing a house with two other people, both of whom worked on the railways. One in particular was known to be quite tough and he was particularly arrogant with it. So we had an ongoing and very competitive series of arm wrestles. He had won one and I had won one. It was a tie.

We ended up down the pub one evening with some friends where we thought we would host the final decider. A crowd had gathered as a lot of pride was at stake.

We began our final arm wrestle. I was absolutely determined to beat this guy – he was so arrogant that I had decided that losing simply was not an option. I was pushing and pushing and pushing and it was paying off as I was winning! I had got his arm right down, his hand was inches from the table – I was about to win – so I went for the final push. I mustered up that winning strength and pushed with all I had left. Suddenly, I heard a deep crack. It was incredibly loud, it sounded like something had smashed.

I looked down at my arm and it was lying on the table in a position that it physically could not have been in. Usually if you've lost an arm wrestle your arm ends up in front and to the right of you. But it was completely distorted; it ended up to the left of me, facing my body in absolutely the wrong place. Then he let go of it. But it stayed on the table. I then noticed that the top of my arm had got much shorter than it was before. I couldn't move it – it was dead weight. The top of my arm, my humerus, was a mess. The bone had snapped and shards of it were visible, it was a spiral break right down the length of the bone. I saw that there were two sharp bits desperately trying to protrude through the skin... I muttered a few words of shock and surprise.

I tried my best to pick the arm up and put it back into position. It didn't hurt at this stage as I was still in a fair amount of shock, it was more bizarre than anything else – it was just like picking up someone else's arm. It is a weird sensation because something that was, moments ago, part of me had become just a lump of meat and bone, resting on the table. I was amazed at how heavy a human arm was, as I tried to push it back into place. An ambulance was called and during the wait the shock dispersed and my arm became unbelievably painful. The muscles began contracting, which was pulling it more and more out of shape, all the while I could feel the bits of bone scraping together inside me.

I held my arm in place as I was taken to hospital where I stayed for two days whilst they were deciding if metal plates and pins should be put in. After long-running disagreements between doctors, they put my arm in a traction plaster. Essentially it is a fairly loose-fitting plaster with a huge weight on the elbow, which pulls the whole thing down. The weight at the elbow, over time, straightens the bone in the upper arm allowing it to heal. It was horrible. I remember a few days later I was on the bus and as it went over bumps in the road and jolted I could still feel the bits of bone grinding against each other.

The doctor said he had actually seen this kind of thing before, apparently it is a relatively common occurrence from arm wrestling; it's a classic injury.

The guy who did it was pleased with himself; he gloated and wouldn't let me hear the end of it. I still don't think he really won, though. It took months to recover and even to this day my arm isn't completely straight. Perhaps it would have been better to have put metal pins in so it might have healed slightly straighter.

I did get a slight revenge on the guy, however. We shared a large Victorian house, which was always creaking and making strange noises. We even spoke before about it being haunted. I was away one weekend and I came back early, without him knowing. I was going to a party so I had dressed in a dinner suit, bow tie and all. I then donned a full-face gorilla mask (with hair and everything). I hid in his wardrobe for some time until he returned to the house. I started making some noises, tapping and scratching in the wardrobe to get him nice and scared. He was with a friend and was getting visibly worried; he was spooked. Just as he began to settle down and take a seat I smashed out of the wardrobe, shouting at the top of my voice as I stormed towards him. He screamed in absolute terror – it could have killed him. He couldn't have imagined there being anyone in the room, especially not a gorilla in a dinner suit.

As revenge it was not quite on a par with my injury, but he was literally shaking even hours later; he was more terrified than I have ever seen anybody before. Suffice to say we didn't have another decider as I think my arm-wrestling days are well and truly over.

# PAUL TAYLOR...

## ... ON ACCIDENTALLY TAKING A HUGE DOSE OF LSD

'We ate, drank, were generally merry and everything was good. Then, very steadily, it wasn't. I had inadvertently ingested a very large dose of Lysergic Acid Diethylamide, or LSD as it's more commonly known, a powerful hallucinogenic Class A drug...'

I am no stranger to recreational drugs. Through my college and university years I experimented with heavy drinking and cannabis, but nothing could have prepared me for that night.

It was a farewell do for a friend of mine who was moving to California. It was 2001 and it was a fantastic evening. My good friend Mark and I arrived at the barbecue nice and early, as we wanted to say our sober goodbyes.

I saw a group of people arrive at the party who I had never seen before; they were visiting the younger brother of the aforementioned friend – the party's host. They seemed like OK people but, from a mile off, it was obvious they were heavily into their drugs. Long hair, scruffy clothes and dopey walks are a dead giveaway.

Anyway, the party rolled on. We ate, drank, were generally merry and everything was good. Then, very steadily, it wasn't. I had inadvertently ingested a very large dose of Lysergic Acid Diethylamide, or LSD as it's more commonly known, a powerful hallucinogenic Class A drug, which was being taken by others at the party. The people I had noticed earlier in the night had put their acid in sugar cubes; this was a method of taking the drug that I was not familiar with, until then. Now I am all too familiar with that procedure.

It was a genuine accident – they had not tricked me. I had simply helped myself to a couple of sugar cubes in a bid to perk myself up a bit. Be careful what you wish for! I still find it strange that they left their drug-laced sugar on a table in the pool house but I can't blame them as I did help myself. As soon as they realised what I had done they were all very supportive, if noticeably excited, but by then it was far too late.

I was meandering around the party, I was slightly tipsy and I was catching up with old friends. Then I had a wave of sickness, of absolute nausea, that literally knocked me off my feet. I sat on the grass, away from the crowds where I took steady deep breaths; naively assuming I had merely eaten a dodgy burger or was coming down with a stomach bug. I felt really bad, so bad I had decided that if these symptoms continued I would phone for a taxi home. A few people asked if I was all right. I lied and told them I was fine and that I just needed some space.

Mark approached me, carrying a handful of beers and a face full of smiles. Drunken friends were not what I needed. By this point my sickness had turned viciously to panic. Something was really wrong. Everything, I mean everything, was a bit further away than it should be. My vision gradually became subtly, but significantly, distorted. My thoughts were quieter than normal, as though the voice in my head was whispering. I was moving away but my surroundings were overwhelming me despite the fact that I continued to sink away from them further. It is impossible to articulate what the sensation was like.

Mark, still by my side, stopped saying words. I could tell he was talking English but, somewhere between his words and my brain, the content lost all meaning. His words were less than sound. I tried to explain my situation, and I think I did, but at the time the same wretched distortion was happening to my vocabulary. My words were bursting with meaning in my head but they materialised as mumbles. At this point I was aware I was not simply ill and that I had taken something.

People began to notice me. I could hear every single person talking concurrently, but clearly. Everything was happening at once but in a timeless and therefore comfortably perceivable way. Sadly, words can't describe how weird it was.

That was enough for me. I stood up, which felt wrong as I had become so familiar with the spot of grass I was sitting on that I genuinely had no concept of another location. What was happening to me? It was far too much to even worry about by now. The fact was, it was happening, it was seriously happening. Perhaps it was a nightmare? Maybe a vision? Was I at the party at all? I walked out of sight.

The property was an expensive mansion, with a pool. I walked past the pool, down a path, through a hedge to the other side of the house, where I sat on a wall. It was nice there – it was quiet and peaceful. But then, gradually, sections of the garden lost their colour and, within moments of me noticing the initial change, everything was sepia.

I closed my eyes, trying to shake the colour back into me. I opened them and it was worse; a vivid purple lens framed my vision. I closed my eyes again and when I opened them the second time the new purple glowed like a thousand suns. It was visually spectacular, but I was too confused to take it in. Despite the colours, I was calm and more aware, but my 'trip' (as it's whimsically referred to) was about to take a turn for the worse.

Insanity is my biggest fear and I was getting a big taste of it. I was scared as well as frustrated. I closed my eyes for a third time. With my eyes shut I could hear the party on the other side of the house. I took a deep breath and opened my eyes once again. I have never panicked so much in my life from what I saw – I was sitting on the same bit of grass, next to Mark and he was asking if I was OK.

Had I even moved? I was close to tears. I stood up, apologised to Mark and left once again. Past the pool and down the path – this was now a very steep hill, so almost a climb. I ran the last part of the journey. I was bloody terrified.

Back to the same wall that was now completely different. This side of the house was not how I remembered it; everything was new. I wondered whether I had actually come here the first time, or had I imagined it? Or had my perception of this place changed somewhere along the line? I sat back on the wall and tried to compose myself.

Again, I foolishly closed my eyes. Vivid colours, distorted shapes and ever-changing images inhabited my mind. Wonderfully artistic pictures of something were in my brain, they were beautiful, incredible things – and then they were something else. One picture became something different before I had time to process the thought of what it was. A fish was soon a bat, which was soon a cow, which was soon a cup, which was then simply blue. Blue was red, green was backwards, red was angry and I was lost. I opened my eyes, with confusion now gripping me tight.

Mark, again... shit. I was back on the grass. Had I moved? Had I been sitting here the whole time, on this same bit of bloody grass? Mark tried to offer me comfort. Or at least he was still making sounds. There was no meaning in his babbling. So I escaped. I thought it would make sense to seek refuge on the other side of the house.

The pool was different and the path was flat. The wall was higher and the world less purple. This was all irrelevant because – you've guessed it – I was still sat on the grass, in the midst of the party. This was not good. I tried again but it kept happening. I was back on the grass. I was in an endless loop of hopeless insanity, and it didn't feel good.

Finally, though, I had honed the skills. I learned the journey, like the back of my hand. By this point I didn't even need to stand up. I could just close my eyes and I would be on the other side of the house. With the blink of an eye I was back at the party.

So now I can teleport? Great! I tried to explain to Mark, who was no longer by my side, so I decided to go and find him.

'Um, Mark's not here,' uttered the host, like these were just words and not the most chilling statement ever spoken in the history of mankind.

I decided I would go and sit back on the grass. This was easy because I was already sat there. Had I moved? I didn't care by this point – I had gone past panic. I wonder now whether I was forgetting the journey each time and was actually just wandering around for hours, or whether it was all in my imagination. I will never know.

But at least when I am on the grass Mark is with me, I thought. I explained my newfound ability to him, but he wasn't listening. He was too busy being purple, or something.

I didn't like him being purple, not one little bit. Purple is a bad colour, I insisted. Why would you have scales if you were purple? I had missed a fundamental point... Why did Mark have scales? He didn't, of course he didn't; he wasn't even there. But his lizard twin was; his horrible reptilian alter ego, which I was growing less fond of by the minute.

I had sparkler trails when I moved my hands but they were no longer my hands, they were just hands. My feet were light years from my head. Mark's new lizard form was not nearly as entertaining as I had first thought. I found it scary by this point.

I thought I had been sat on that one piece of grass for hours. Why was it not dark yet? It was still dusk. 'What a lovely sunset,' I thought to myself. I couldn't see it, though; I could smell it, hear it and feel it. Vision was no longer reliable, as Lizard-Boy had demonstrated.

My body was gone. Just sensations, colours, confusion and the rest is no more than a dream. The remainder of the evening is a series of confusing memories, none of which are reliable. The kind of memories you get after a weird dream, where you wonder how much was actually in the dream and how much you simply added later when you tried to remember.

Everything was calm when I woke. I was lying in the pool house with the druggies I saw the night before. They explained everything, which they thoroughly enjoyed doing. I was relieved to see Mark. He said that I kept accusing him of being a – and I'll never forget his exact words –'purple, turtle-faced teleport wizard'. He had misunderstood as he was in fact a lizard and I was the teleport wizard.

It was an evening that I will never forget. My overall experience was negative, but I don't regret it. I will, however, never touch hallucinogenic drugs again.

# MARK CALL...

## ... ON THE AVALANCHE THAT NEARLY KILLED HIM

'Suddenly I found myself alternately sliding and tumbling, I had little idea which way was up – I was at the mercy of an avalanche. Bright light, greyness, more light. I kept my mouth closed, as I remembered that, bizarrely, suffocation from inhaling snow is a common cause of death in avalanches. I got on my front and tried again to stop myself with an ice axe; useless.'

It was a grey Sunday morning in early June when I was caught by an avalanche while climbing with a friend near Chamonix in the French Alps. We should have died but were given another chance at life.

It was the end of a good week climbing in the Chamonix massif – a ten by twenty mile mass of granite mountains that has drawn climbers from around the world for over 150 years. My climbing partner Kevin and I are both experienced climbers – a holiday activity that many find hard to understand. But despite being well-experienced and well-equipped for high

Alpine snow and ice climbing, the elements and chance had more of a bearing on whether we lived or died.

At 7.30 a.m. we had begun our descent of Mont Blanc du Tacul, the north face, which was loaded with snow and known for its avalanche risk. But we had no choice; it was the only way off the mountain.

It was slow-going in the deep soft snow, but we were a quarter of the way down – so far, so good. With a tight fifty-metre rope between us, Kevin and I began traversing a wide snow slope. Without warning or sound, a huge slab of snow broke away and headed off down the north face with us in it. I can still see the fracture line snaking rapidly from my footstep across the face.

The conditions were too dangerous for the rescue service to send people. The mobile phone brought false comfort – the voice of someone sitting in warmth and safety seemed close and yet so far away. The Apollo 13 astronauts must have felt something similar. We were on our own. But how did we get ourselves into this mess?

It started with the optimism, euphoria even, of another climb. On Friday we had squeezed our way past the tourists just outside the little ice cave on the Aiguille du Midi, a peak which towers over the climbing Mecca of Chamonix, which is reached by the highest cable car in Europe. Closing the gate to which is fixed the sign, 'Danger – Alpinists Only', we descended the narrow, steep snow ridge to enter the realm of rock, snow and ice.

Although conscious that we were in a world, just like the sea or desert, where humans are visitors, we were confident we brought the skills and experience to carry us successfully through the challenge ahead. As we plodded along we spoke of that uplifting joy that comes from getting back into the high mountains. It might be devoid of green or permanent life, but it's pure and beautiful and it felt like a privilege to be there again.

Our objective was the Kuffner Ridge on the Mont Maudit – part of the massive lump of granite that is Mont Blanc. We made our way across the glaciers and climbed to a small mountain hut perched on the ridge where we spent the night.

We left the little refuge at 4.30 a.m. and began the route. It was classic Alpine climbing; starting as an undulating ridge of alternating snow and rock bastions. At times we walked on the exposed snow ridge; at others we were front pointing on hard old ice with the aggressive-looking crampons that adorned our boots, or we were picking our way up fractured rock. All was going well and we reached the summit of the ridge on the shoulder of the mountain around midday. Here we got our first inkling of trouble. Having been climbing on the east of the Massif, the weather coming in from the west had been hidden from us. Now, though, sickly grey clouds were coming to fill in what had previously been a vault of blue.

After descending the snow slopes of Mont Maudit, we were ready to leave the lonelier path of our harder route for descent on the Mont Blanc *voie normale*. This is the normal route taken by those doing the climb to Mont Blanc via the three 'monts' – Mont Blanc de Tacul, Mont Maudit and Mont Blanc itself. As many as a hundred people will complete this feat of endurance in good weather during the summer months. This should have meant that there would have been a well-trodden track to follow, which would have taken us down the tricky north face of the Tacul – a straightforward journey taking three to four hours in *good* weather.

The storm had arrived. The gusts were so strong that we needed to crouch occasionally to avoid being blown over. The spindrift of blown snow brought images from Attenborough documentaries on the Arctic. Only this time we were the penguins shuffling across the ice cap.

The part of this route that changes regularly is the section that descends the north face of the Tacul. An 800 m face of steep snow punctuated by shattered seracs – great blocks of ice that represent the end of a glacier obstructing our path. This is where we had hoped to find traces of a route, which promised safety and a hasty exit from that area. Serac fall was certainly a risk, although we were to find that the face held other dangers.

We were unable to find the track, so we tried to follow the terrain by going over the wide shoulder and turning north-easterly. The visibility was poor and the wind was biting but gusts gave us occasional glimpses of ten or twenty metres ahead. We found a line feature and followed it, reasoning that it could be a trace of the *voie normale*. Then my right leg sank up to the thigh, while my left remained on the hard ice. Extracting myself, I heard a shout from Kevin who had done the same thing ten metres behind me. We had been following the lower lip of a small crevasse and put our right and uphill legs through the fragile snow covering.

In the fading light we had only one option: to dig a snow hole and get out of the wind that was blasting us with driven snow. After two hours of digging and scraping with a small aluminium pan, we were able to crawl into our home for the night.

The night dragged slowly on as we wiggled our fingers and toes. I reflected that it is not just the fact that there are those out there that you love but also that they love you that's important. In a situation like this, a little validation goes a long way. I was determined that my life was not going to end like that and I stubbornly resolved to get off that bloody mountain.

Eventually dawn came and with it a clearing in the weather. The wind had died and the snow had stopped. Kevin and I emerged from the snow hole and we both excavated the area for our bags and gear that were buried under the snow. By then it was clear that there was maybe 80 cm of new snow; beautiful light powder. Oh, for skis!

We began our descent of the snow-laden north face of the Tacul, knowing we were walking on eggshells. The slope is famed for being at the critical angle for avalanches, making it like a gun with a hair trigger.

Suddenly I found myself alternately sliding and tumbling, I had little idea which way was up – I was at the mercy of an avalanche. Bright light, greyness, more light. I kept my mouth closed, as I remembered that, bizarrely, suffocation from inhaling snow is a common cause of death in avalanches. I got on my front and tried again to stop myself with an ice axe; useless. I tried to put a foot down, but it dug in and ended up under my armpit. Another few spins and I was on my front again, on a harder base of ice or hard snow and I began to slow down. I tried to put my spread feet down and my crampons started to bite. I was just beginning to think I might be able to stop when another wall of snow hit me and off we went again.

Despite the chaos, my mind stayed clear. I calmly said to myself that I should expect a bump that will end it one way or the other. And that this would probably be a case of 'Game Over'. Then I was aware of being weightless. That was a possibility that I hadn't considered. I distinctly recall thinking in a detached way, 'that's not good'. Now I was expecting an even bigger bump, but it didn't come. As abruptly as it started, it was over. I was lying on my back, on the surface and

I looked over to my left and saw Kevin two metres away. Our rope was buried in the snow but we were both on top.

I reflected on what had just happened in the previous packed seconds and made a mental note to buy a lottery ticket. We had been lucky beyond measure. I have never felt less in control of an outcome.

After tumbling 200 metres with the avalanche we had gone over an ice cliff and fallen twenty-five metres vertically and by some extraordinary luck we landed on a ledge or ridge of snow, which had been softened by the snow of our avalanche. If we had landed just a little further out we would have carried on down the ever-steepening slope, another 1,000 m to certain death, and if we had landed just short of our spot we would have fallen down a crevasse.

While we had survived against the odds we were now in the middle of a north face of steep snow and embedded ice blocks. It was to take us a further eight hours to climb down to the Refuge des Cosmiques, a manned mountain hut with beds, warmth and food. Given the impossible conditions for a rescue, it wouldn't have helped to know at the time that I had actually fractured five vertebrae, including a compression fracture that would put me in a rigid corset for three months.

The next day the helicopter rescue service was able to pick us up and take us to hospital. Waiting in the A & E reception of Sallanches Hospital we mused over climbing risks. With the customary denial of climbers we separated out the objective risk and concluded that an injury such as this could happen falling off a ladder. Climbers don't seek danger in a Russian roulette way; but they recognise it and seek to manage it with skills and some degree of caution and self-restraint. But they don't say 'it couldn't happen to me'; because they know it could.

Ten minutes later, a man was wheeled in on a trolley. The nurses anxiously discussed his symptoms with the paramedics. He had hurt his back and couldn't feel his hands or feet and it looked serious. As I listened with new-found solidarity, I heard that he had fallen off a ladder whilst repairing his roof. 'I'm lucky,' I thought to myself.

Recovery brought its own challenges. After a week in hospital there began ten weeks in a rigid orthopaedic corset, in which I could either stand or lie but not sit. I had plenty of time to reflect on what this experience meant to me.

Of course, there are practical lessons learned from the 'epic' – as climbers call an outing that didn't go quite according to plan. The value of a trusted partner, the importance of skills beyond which you think you will need, like remembering how to use a compass or dig a snow hole; the importance of belief in survival; keeping a level head and knowing when to stop and when to go on. Perhaps above all, having respect for the weather and allowing a proper time margin around it.

On a deeper level, it would be nice to say that I was struck by a revelation. That the answer to the question of what to do with my life came bursting into my consciousness. But it didn't. I am not a fatalist, nor am I spiritual or even religious. Nevertheless, it has changed me. Perhaps in ways I don't yet understand. It seems ironic that it takes death or a brush with it to make us think about life.

Only when you are faced with the real prospect of not living does life seem such a wonderful gift. Of course, it shouldn't be like that. Trite sayings spring to mind – 'today is the first day of the rest of your life' – sentiments that we laugh off or ignore in our busyness. For myself I feel differently about life but am still trying to come to terms with how. I think I am more tolerant and don't complain about the little things as much. I'm also less critical of others.

I have a new determination to do some of the things that I have put off, like trying to write that book or take that journey I have wanted to do since boyhood.

But I think for me the most significant change is that I am more accepting of who I am. I have in the past always been striving to do more, get more, be somewhere different – in short to be someone different. I am more content just to be me.

Should a near-death experience make you accept your lot or say to yourself that you won't put up with things you don't like? Should you be more accepting or more demanding? There is, of course, no answer, or at least no answer that fits everyone. The important thing is to think. Happiness is, they say, a journey rather than a destination. At least we should travel with our eyes open.

# ACKNOWLEDGEMENTS

A special thanks to all those who have helped me throughout the production of this book, especially to each and every person who has been kind enough to give up their time and share their story with such honesty – without you there would be no book.

I struggle to think of any other scenario where I would be tasked to find such a diverse selection of British people and learn so much from them, so I am grateful to Summersdale for this opportunity. I am also indebted to Camelot's press team for their impressive assistance; to Neil Forsyth for his kindness; to both the *Alton Post Gazette* and the *Alton Herald* for running articles for me and to my parents whose support and guidance during this project has been nothing short of priceless.

**Benedict Allen**
www.benedictallen.com

**Ian Colquhoun**
www.iancolquhoun.org.uk

**Kerri-Ann Cartwright**

**Dave Heeley**
www.blinddaveheeley.co.uk

**Kelly Green**
kellog44@gmail.com

**Neil Forsyth for his help with John Rose's story**
www.neilforsyth.com

**Beverli Rhodes**
www.shaman-beverli-rhodes.blogspot.com

**Sinclair Beecham**
www.hoxtonhotels.com

**Michelle Bowater**
www.wlsgroup.co.uk

**David Tait**
www.davidtait.com
www.nspcc.org.uk

**Craig Green**

**Ann Down**

**David Stone**
davidstone78@gmail.com

**Kayt Webster-Brown**
www.vertical-lines.com

# ACKNOWLEDGEMENTS

**Martin Jones**
mjonestraining@blueyonder.co.uk

**Eric Colon**

**Siobhan Peal**
www.talkingwithcapricorn.com

**Matthew Wood-Hill**
mwoodhill@hotmail.co.uk

**Valerie Austin**
www.valerieaustin.com

**Lawrence Ford**

**Mark Call**
mark@markcall.co.uk

Have you enjoyed this book? If so, why not write a review
on your favourite website?

Thanks very much for buying this Summersdale book.

# www.summersdale.com